Good Science

Good Science is an account of psychological research emphasizing the moral foundations of inquiry. This volume brings together existing disciplinary critiques of scientism, objectivism, and instrumentalism, and then discusses how these contribute to institutionalized privilege and to less morally responsive research practices. The author draws on historical, critical, feminist, and science studies traditions to provide an alternative account of psychological science and to highlight the irreducibly moral foundations of everyday scientific practice. This work outlines a theoretical framework for thinking about and practicing psychology in ways that center moral responsibility, collective commitment, and justice. The book then applies this framework, describing psychological research practices in terms of the their moral dilemmas. Also included are materials meant to aid in methods instruction and mentoring.

JOSHUA W. CLEGG is Associate Professor of Psychology at John Jay College of Criminal Justice, City University of New York (CUNY), and a member of the faculty in the Critical Social and Personality Psychology doctoral program at the Graduate Center, CUNY. He has published widely on history, methods, and epistemology in the social sciences.

Good Science

Psychological Inquiry as Everyday Moral
Practice

JOSHUA W. CLEGG
John Jay College of Criminal Justice, CUNY

CAMBRIDGE
UNIVERSITY PRESS

CAMBRIDGE
UNIVERSITY PRESS

University Printing House, Cambridge CB2 8BS, United Kingdom

One Liberty Plaza, 20th Floor, New York, NY 10006, USA

477 Williamstown Road, Port Melbourne, VIC 3207, Australia

314–321, 3rd Floor, Plot 3, Splendor Forum, Jasola District Centre,
New Delhi – 110025, India

103 Penang Road, #05–06/07, Visioncrest Commercial, Singapore 238467

Cambridge University Press is part of the University of Cambridge.

It furthers the University's mission by disseminating knowledge in the pursuit of
education, learning, and research at the highest international levels of excellence.

www.cambridge.org
Information on this title: www.cambridge.org/9781316519752
DOI: 10.1017/9781009022217

© Cambridge University Press 2022

This publication is in copyright. Subject to statutory exception
and to the provisions of relevant collective licensing agreements,
no reproduction of any part may take place without the written
permission of Cambridge University Press.

First published 2022

A catalogue record for this publication is available from the British Library.

Library of Congress Cataloging-in-Publication Data
Names: Clegg, Joshua W., author.
Title: Good science : psychological inquiry as everyday moral practice / Joshua W. Clegg.
Description: Cambridge, United Kingdom ; New York, NY : Cambridge University Press,
    2022. | Includes bibliographical references and index.
Identifiers: LCCN 2021019845 (print) | LCCN 2021019846 (ebook) | ISBN
    9781316519752 (hardback) | ISBN 9781009011129 (paperback) | ISBN
    9781009022217 (epub)
Subjects: LCSH: Psychology–Research–Methodology–History. | Psychology–Moral and
    ethical aspects.
Classification: LCC BF76.5 .C54 2022 (print) | LCC BF76.5 (ebook) | DDC 150.72–dc23
LC record available at https://lccn.loc.gov/2021019845
LC ebook record available at https://lccn.loc.gov/2021019846

ISBN 978-1-316-51975-2 Hardback
ISBN 978-1-009-01112-9 Paperback

Cambridge University Press has no responsibility for the persistence or accuracy
of URLs for external or third-party internet websites referred to in this publication
and does not guarantee that any content on such websites is, or will remain,
accurate or appropriate.

To Jill, Afton, and Henry, with love and gratitude.

Contents

Preface

I have been writing this book for fifteen years. I've done other things along the way, but most of those – almost every professional presentation or publication – have been connected in some way to the ideas presented in this book. I have felt an urgency to make some sense of science in psychology, at first just for myself, then later for my students and other friends, and this has patterned all of my work.

That urgency came upon me almost from the first psychology course that I took as an undergraduate. Then, and since, I have felt a vague unease about the discipline; one that I have been trying, variously, to name, exorcise, diagnose, or remedy. At first, I took that unease to be primarily epistemological. There seemed to be too many contradictions, inconsistencies, and half-formed notions in writing about science, research, and method in psychology. Over time, however, I have learned that this is not so unusual; that, actually, we all have a hard time writing sensibly about science. Science is composed of a vast history, made up of radically distinct epistemic, disciplinary, cultural, and geographic regionalities. It is hardly surprising if any one of us can only lay an imperfect hold of some small part of that geography.

In trying to lay hold of my own small part of the science story, I have realized that my unease was not primarily, or at least not essentially, epistemological; rather, it was a *moral* unease. I felt that there was often something *wrong* about how psychologists talked about (and sometimes deployed) science; not wrong in the sense that we were mistaken or we misunderstood science (though that may also be true), but wrong in the sense that we seemed to be trying to extract psychological science from its moral context. We seemed to be imagining a science ruled entirely by technique; a science protected from political interest, bias, or values; a purely objective science that could legitimate particular forms of political and moral action, without the need for any political or moral justification.

This never felt *right* to me. It often felt, in fact, like a kind of epistemological bullying, where those in positions of influence within psychology could enforce their interests and worldviews by signaling their methodological purity. There is no question that, historically speaking, this is exactly what many (though, I trust, not most) psychologists have done – that is, they have used the authority of science to justify and protect racist, sexist, classist, ableist, and homophobic ideologies and policies (more on that in the body of the text).

In studying that history, and in reading the work of many brilliant theorists and critics of science and of psychology, I have found names and vocabularies for my unease. What I have found is a disciplinary discourse, grounded in a basically objectivist philosophy, that obscures the moral foundations of science and so allows those who can afford to deploy the machinery of the discipline to disguise their moral commitments and so avoid moral accountability for them.

Over the last fifteen years, I have stumbled through various accounts of this objectivist ideology and its accompanying social machinery. Along the way, I have developed what I hope is a clearer understanding of what psychological science is really like and what is really at stake there. Also along the way, I have felt the need to better explain all of this to my students, and so better prepare them for the discipline they are joining.

This book is the fruit of that stumbling and striving. I have tried to honestly and rigorously account for psychological research in a way that centers, rather than obscures, the moral foundations of science, and my hope is that this will help readers reveal and refine, in their research, teaching, and writing, the moral commitments driving psychological research. This is, I think, what it means to do *good science*.

Acknowledgments

This book owes a great deal to a great many. I would like to thank them here without any implication that they might be responsible for the mistakes or excesses of the text. My many mentors, including Brent Slife and Jaan Valsiner, helped me know what to read and how to write. The ideas, scholarship, and friendship of the brilliant scholars in Divisions 24 and 26 of the American Psychological Association lie behind at least every other word in this book. This includes Kate Slaney and the wonderful folks at Simon Fraser University who hosted me during the sabbatical year when I wrote much of this book. And, especially, my long-time friends and collaborators Brady Wiggins and Joe Ostenson. The faculty and students in the Critical Social and Personality Psychology and Environmental Psychology programs at the City University of New York Graduate Center also, probably often unknowingly, vetted every idea in this book. I especially want to thank those students who so often listened to and shaped these ideas – Karyna, Fernando, Chris, Rachel, Emese, Liz, Donald, and Kate. I also want to acknowledge the many John Jay College master's students whose thoughtful, serious, and heartfelt responses to discussions, readings, and exercises in my research methods classes have inspired and refined many of the ideas in this book. I want to thank Cambridge University Press; I searched hard for a publisher that I could feel good about and their principled approach to publishing and open access made the search easy. Finally, I want to acknowledge the contributions of my wonderful family - my parents who taught me to love reading and thinking, and Jill, Afton, and Henry, who taught me the meaning of life.

Introduction

When psychologists write about how to do science, we[1] mostly devote our time to the technical elements of data collection and analysis. A guiding assumption in this book is that these technical elements are relatively minor considerations in the prosecution of good science. This is not to say that they are unimportant, but only that they are regional concerns within a much larger scientific geography whose principal contours are not technical nor procedural, but social and moral.[2]

I think it uncontroversial to claim that, like everyone else, the scientist navigates a world of moral choices, human relationships, and political systems that shape and constrain the kinds of work it is possible to do. The scientist must make difficult, inherently ambiguous choices about who and what matters (e.g., is worthy of study), where to make compromises and accept constraints, what counts as evidence, and so on. The scientist must also attend to an often vast network of relationships – with supervisors, administrative staff, collaborators, research participants, journal editors, policy makers, and so on – through which her work is fashioned and disseminated. And that work is bound up in a range of political systems she must navigate, including institutions that hold legal or financial interest, those that provide auxiliary support and oversight, those that administer local resources and responsibilities, and those that arbitrate disciplinary influence and prestige.

---

[1] In this book, I will often make use of collective pronouns (i.e., "we" and "our") in discussing psychological research. I do this to highlight my role as a practicing psychological researcher and not as an outside commentator. I take all of the arguments and analyses presented in this book as applying to me, to my students, and to my colleagues. From my perspective, we are all in this together.

[2] Throughout this book, I will very often use the term "moral" (and its cognates). I employ this term in a broad way to encompass all questions of the good, right, and just. When I am talking about science and psychology as everyday moral practices, I mean that these practices are anchored in ideas about, and commitments to, right action.

Every working scientist knows and navigates this world of choices, relationships, and institutions, but this is generally not what we talk about in research methods texts and courses and certainly not the terms by which we account for or warrant scientific claims. Our habit, rather, is to write, talk, and teach as though a small set of narrowly defined technical "methods" for collecting and analyzing data are what constitute science.

There may be good reasons for this habit. The real complexities of science as practiced are not easily conveyed in the short page lengths and time frames available to the writer and teacher. And, in any case, the vast tacit dimensions of science are absorbed primarily through mentored practice and not through the study of *post hoc* descriptions. Methods descriptions, rather, function as a kind of shorthand for the activities of scientists, with the full-bodied details of real practice supplied either from experience or from the imaginations of other scientists already familiar with them. More textured, descriptively complete accounts of science (of the sort, for example, that you find in sociological and historical studies of science) are clearly not necessary to train technically capable research-ers, nor to convey the intent and substance of one scientist's work to another.

To put it colloquially, we figure it out – novices figure out the things they weren't taught or didn't fully understand and other researchers figure out (or, really, assume) those things left out of a research report. Time and space constraints (in both the teaching and reporting of research) require us to make choices about what we will leave out of any research account and these constraints are such that we will have to leave out nearly everything. A research project is a tightly woven fabric of small human moments that no report and no text can adequately convey. I don't contest these limits and don't pretend that researchers can or should explicate the full human scope of their activities. But there are good reasons to turn more of our attention to the social and moral contours of these activities and real dangers in ignoring them.

At the very least, the moral contours of research practice merit attention because these can have profound consequences for the dis-cipline, as well as for those affected by psychological research. Visible to all, for example, are the damaging effects of researcher misconduct, with cases of fabricated data or participant abuse creating mistrust in the status and intentions of psychological science. Also damaging are the countless examples of scientific work (in psychology and out) in the service of oppression, injustice, and harm. Too often, psychologists have been on the side of the powerful, the aggressor, the oppressor (supporting apartheid in South Africa, eugenic programs across the world, torture in the Bush-era USA, etc.) and too often we have hidden those allegiances behind the neutrality of science. Too often psychologists have chosen to dehumanize, manipulate, instrumentalize, and outright harm and it is not a coincidence that we have also too often chosen to ignore the political and moral dimensions of research. The rhetorical retreat into objectivism is a thin veneer for our history of compromised allegiances.

But even if the history of psychological research were a sunny catalogue of human good, in need of no particular oversight, accounts of research divorced from its moral and political context are also insufficient on purely descriptive and epistemic grounds. What I am suggesting in this book is that science as a whole is best understood, and most responsibly and effectively practiced, from the perspective of its moral, social, and political context. We mistake science when we talk of it as a technical method, not just because there is no general set of rules, techniques, or assumptions that uniquely define science (Feyerabend, 1993), but because science as practiced is much more a community than a particular set of techniques. Science is a delicate human system, completely dependent on the trust, good faith, and consensus shared between particular scientists and within the much larger network of support that makes science possible. The integrity of this human system is the integrity of science.

Thus, the most important reason to frame science in terms of everyday moral practices is because such practices *are* science; they are its shape and attending to the obligations inherent within them is the substance of doing *good* science. Among these contours are those that shape best practices for designing and conducting data collection and analysis, but these best practices (i.e., traditional "research methods") cannot be defensibly considered independent of the people and institutions that constitute them (and thus universal and value-neutral), nor as the full and final arbiters of scientific work or truth. They are one set of considerations to which a scientist must attend, but they do not constitute science. Good science comes in and from particular persons paying careful attention to the whole range of moral choices, human relationships, and social institutions through which everyday science work is done.

The aim of this book is to provide researchers with a framework for understanding and practicing science in terms of this careful moral attentiveness. In Part I of the book, I outline the most basic ways that traditional notions of objectivity, science, and ethics must be reframed for this moral attentiveness to be possible. This "reframing" is not at all original and has roots older than the discipline, so I present it in the character of a critical summary.

In Chapter 1, I discuss scientism, or the belief that scientific knowledge is the most (or only) legitimate form of knowledge. My argument is that scientism mischaracterizes science as an epistemically privileged and unified method. Actual scientific practice, however, has demonstrated tremendous variability in theory and method across time, place, and disciplinary context, and can best be understood as a historically contingent human activity. Drawing on historical and philosophical critiques, I characterize scientism as a kind of science fundamentalism that insulates scientists from social and moral critique and so contributes to the institutionalization of exceptionalism and privilege. I discuss elements of scientism in professional psychology, using historical and contemporary examples to show that it is a common (perhaps even a majority) position.

In Chapter 2, I discuss theories of objectivism, or the requirement that all genuine knowledge be observer-independent and (or) neutral. I provide a brief outline of objectivist accounts and distinguish these from objectivity. Drawing on historical analyses, I show how objectivity in science refers to a set of practices aimed at reducing variability in the recording and transmission of observations, but that objectivism is an overgeneralization of these practices into an incoherent epistemological mandate. I argue that objectivism is illusory, both because knowledge can never be produced independent of a historically situated knower and also because neither individuals nor human systems can be neutral. Objectivism, I claim, can only be performative and so serves as a cover for, rather than a defense against, institutionalized forms of privilege. Objectivist practices also dehumanize the subjects of scientific labor and so anesthetize the moral responsiveness of those who produce and consume research.

In Chapter 3, I discuss scientific instrumentalism, or the notion that scientific findings are morally neutral and that scientific activities are justified primarily in terms of their pragmatic utility. I argue that an instrumentalist approach to psychology disguises the moral and political agendas of those who deploy psychological research, conflating these with a neutralist account of "what works." I provide a broad historical sketch of those for whom psychology has worked – primarily, large institutions – and of those for whom psychology has not worked – principally, those in disenfranchised social positions. I detail some of the most egregious examples of harm, exploitation, and injustice in the history of psychology, providing a general analysis of the ways that psychologists have encoded racism, sexism, and other forms of prejudice under seemingly neutral categories like intelligence.

Speaking very generally, Part I of this book draws on a long critical tradition to argue that scientism, objectivism, and instrumentalism have functioned both to strategically dehumanize persons and to provide a "neutralist" veneer for morally destructive practices. To be clear, this is a critique of an overgeneralized metaphysical program (objectivism, scientism, and instrumentalism) and not of the more local traditions that have lent it authority. In other words, it is not a critique of objectivity – which is a set of very useful practices whose purpose is to reduce variability in the recording and reporting of observations – but of objectivism, which casts all true knowledge as context and observer-independent. Likewise, this is not a critique of science, but an attempt to disentangle science from the shallow dogmas of scientism – that is, the insistence that science is the transparent and final arbiter of all truth.

In Part II of the book, I draw on contemporary philosophy of science, and critical, feminist, and science studies scholarship to move beyond the critique of objectivist frameworks and toward an account of psychological science as actually practiced.

In Chapter 4, I draw on social science, historical, and philosophical studies of science to describe the everyday activities involved in science. I characterize the core scientific task as the production of accounts that legitimate, organize, and mobilize scientific labor. These accounts are shaped by a complex network of social constraints and processes. Through the main body of the chapter, I describe some of these constraints and processes, including those cultural and political (e.g., national funding priorities), professional and disciplinary (disciplinary norms concerning methods, equipment, writing conventions, etc.), institutional (e.g., managing the requirements of bureaucracies and budgets), local and interpersonal (e.g., lab politics and professional rivalries), and dispositional and personal (e.g., personal talents and capacities for science work). I argue that these various social constraints and processes constitute the moral geography of science and that to navigate them well and responsibly is the substance of good science.

In Chapter 5, I extend the social and moral account of scientific work with a similarly social and moral account of scientific justification. My argument is that scientific justification should consist, not simply in the construction of evidentiary rationales, but in the refinement of the whole moral architecture of science. I insist that the "core competency" in training and oversight for psychological inquiry should be the justification – that is, the making just, right, and true – of research practices. Drawing on the work of Emmanuel Levinas and Helen Longino (among others), I argue that two forms of practice essential to such justification are an open disciplinary politics, or an institutionalized openness to uncertainty, critique, and correction by the widest possible range of qualified contributors, and a committed research praxis, or an approach to research where everyday scientific practices are interrogated and refined to become consistent with explicit values.

In Chapter 6, I discuss the practices conducive to an open disciplinary politics. I critique rhetorics of certainty in science (and psychology), characterizing these as dogmatic and antithetical to good science, and contrasting them with the humility, skepticism, and openness required for healthy scientific inquiry. My claim is that such openness can only occur when the broadest possible range of qualified contributors have equal standing to challenge scientific claims and practices, particularly those reflective of historical and structural inequalities. I discuss some practices conducive to such openness, focusing on recommendations from decolonizing and feminist traditions, including the centering of historical and cultural critiques of science and the privileging of marginalized and oppressed perspectives in publishing, governance, and hiring decisions. Practices like these, I argue, are integral to an open disciplinary politics, and they only become possible through active epistemic citizenship aimed at transforming disciplinary structures and practices.

In Chapter 7, I describe a committed research praxis where scientists strive to articulate the community-level value commitments that define good science, and to evaluate the degree to which particular scientific activities and products reflect those commitments. I argue that one primary way for psychologists to engage in this sort of committed praxis is by asking questions together in a place. That is, we can subject our work to insistent moral attention through collective and locally situated forms of reflection and responsibility. I suggest that these forms could include reflexivity, transparency, participatory and community-oriented research practices, political, historical, and material analyses of our research traditions and products, resistance to overgeneralized and "scaled" forms of neoliberal management, and other practices that help anchor research work to the local and communal commitments that justify it.

Speaking generally, the aim of Part II is to frame the practices of psychological research in terms of their social, moral, and historical foundations, and to point toward a similarly social and moral account of scientific *justification*. I use the word *justify* here with intention. Those who write about scientific justification have generally treated it as a sort of defensive maneuver – as the construction of evidentiary rationales – but this is an echo of an objectivist tradition that I have no wish to defend. Here, I point instead toward an older set of meanings – one where justification is about justice, about making just our practices, relationships, and systems. It is not coincidental that our truth words are also moral words and I argue here that this relationship is primordial, formative, and indissoluble; that there is no separating being right and upright; truth and being true; conscience and science. Justifying psychological research is thus about justifying the social and moral architecture of particular scientific communities, an endeavor, I argue, that requires both a disciplinary commitment to open political structures and more local commitments to explicit, community-driven values.

In the simplest terms, my argument in Part II is that good science is a matter of individual and collective moral attention, something that I attempt to model in Part III of the book. In each of the chapters in Part III, I frame the research endeavor in terms of particular choices the researcher must make, relationships that she must attend to, and social systems and structures within which she must work.

In Chapter 8, I discuss some of the most salient moral questions, dilemmas, and duties involved in choosing a research community (and conversation) in which to participate. Conducting research in some area, I argue, is not so much a solitary domain choice as a process of becoming socialized to a particular community and to its values, languages, traditions, institutions, and ways of thinking, writing, and working. In some measure, this also means becoming responsible for those traditions and values. I also discuss the ways that participating in a research community involves building the relationships of trust and good faith upon which all science rests, a relational process requiring honesty, the nurturing of cooperative relationships, and other duties. I also emphasize the political, institutional, and economic forces that structure research communities and the necessity of active epistemic citizenship to transform these in ways that serve the collective values of those communities.

In Chapter 9, I outline some of the most important moral considerations involved in the design and conduct of research. I first discuss research funding, emphasizing conflicts between resource limitations and epistemic and moral values. I then discuss research space considerations, framing these in terms of dwelling practices that express our commitments (to hospitality, conservation, etc.) and that shape our communities and environments. Next, I discuss the moral affordances of research equipment, arguing that such equipment is not just a set of neutral tools but a way of extending and transforming our individual and collective embodiment. I then discuss how organizing research entails a moral ordering (of priorities and persons) set amid a micropolitics of local power relationships. Finally, I discuss some of the moral dilemmas involved in soliciting and managing research participation, focusing on the duties to cultivate the choice, voice, and safety of all who participate in research.

In Chapter 10, I discuss the moral context of research interpretation and reporting. I describe interpretation as the constitution of evidence within an epistemic frame, characterized by the totality of (always at least partly moral) commitments underlying analytic choices. These analytic choices include those concerning what is worthy of study, what kinds of methods and forms of evidence are considered acceptable, and what kinds of claims are warrantable. I also emphasize the ways that evidence is not merely gathered or reported, but constituted within a rhetorical and political context. In the latter half of the chapter, I discuss the moral affordances of research reporting, focusing on questions of fairness, honesty, representation, and other considerations involved in report authoring. I focus specifically on questions of:

collaboration and credit; style and representation; venue, availability, and audience; submission, editorial, and revision; and the dissemination and use of research reports.

As I consider these lived elements of research, I outline important moral, social, and political questions and dilemmas that must be addressed. My contention is that in addressing research from this moral and political perspective, we will, in fact, be doing the most that we can to fulfill the obligation of creating good, truly justifiable, science.

In Chapter 11, I summarize the book as a whole, arguing that the dilemmas, decisions, relational and institutional commitments, and other moral considerations described here are the essence of good science. I also argue that, because a social and moral account of science does not ignore nor hide the human and moral contexts of research, it subjects scientific claims to a more rigorous scrutiny than does an objectivist account and so strengthens the warrant for those claims. Finally, I discuss how the account offered in this book impacts everyday psychological practice, acknowledging the inevitably local and contextual ways that a moral accounting of psychology might be realized within specific research communities. This caveat notwithstanding, I suggest that anyone could begin by asking, in their own communities, the kinds of questions posed here as well as by participating in an epistemic activism aimed at transforming disciplinary structures and practices.

Following the final chapter of the book, I provide, in Appendix A , a detailed *Instructor's Guide*. This guide includes a brief essay on methods instruction in psychology, and a discussion of ways to use the chapters and sections of this book in methods instruction and mentoring. In Appendix B, I include a detailed curriculum, based on a Master's-level introductory research methods course, integrating concepts and readings from the book. In Appendix C, I outline a list of dilemmas common in research design, accompanied by a set of questions meant to inspire moral reflection about those dilemmas (a resource that could be useful in mentored research).

PART I

Clearing the Ground

I don't necessarily *want* to begin this book with an involved critique of scientism or objectivism. The job has been done and more than once.[1] Yet here I am, marshalling my wits and courage. I feel the need to pick the same old fights mostly because psychologists (and other scientists) are, from our earliest education, inoculated with a set of immunities against a moral understanding of our work. That moral understanding is, I think, quite straightforward; it is easy to see how and why we have particular responsibilities to particular persons and communities at particular moments in scientific practice. But these particularities of moral responsibility are dismantled and obscured by a scientistic education. So much so that what should be obvious and second nature – namely, that science is a community, and that good science means personal integrity and principled commitment, moral responsibility to, and care for, particular persons, and good citizenship – is, at best, an invisible background assumption and, at worst, a simply alien way of thinking about science.

Part I of this book is thus the story of how we are encouraged to become insensible to the deepest meanings and obligations of science work. I tell this story in three parts. In Chapter 1, I outline the basic assumptions of scientism and show how these are more a kind of science fundamentalism than a faithful reflection of science as actually practiced. I try to show how scientism encourages epistemic exceptionalism and so insulates researchers, including psychologists, from criticism and from genuine moral reflection about the practices and products of research.

I continue my critique of traditional science education in psychology with a discussion, in Chapter 2, of objectivism. I argue that the objectivist account of science overgeneralizes the notion of objectivity into an unfulfillable epistemological mandate for person-independent

---

[1] And certainly better than I will be able to manage here.

and neutral knowledge. I suggest that because objectivism is purely performative (i.e., a pretense), it serves as a cover for institutionalized privilege. I also try to show how objectivism leads to attitudes and practices that have the potential to dehumanize psychological subjects (or to simply delegitimize them as moral subjects), and also to anesthetize the moral responsiveness of researchers. I conclude Part I with a critique, in Chapter 3, of instrumental logics in psychology. I argue that because such logics cast research as a largely pragmatic affair whose findings serve everyone equally, they obscure the moral and political agendas of those who deploy psychological research. I try to show how these often invisible agendas have patterned psychology with a history of exploitation, injustice, and harm.

This three-part critique of science as typically understood within accounts of psychological research is meant to show not simply the epistemological limitations of scientism, objectivism, and instrumentalism, but also to illuminate how these traditions of understanding obscure and even undermine the moral responsibilities of psychological researchers. And this is why I raise the bones of our ancient enmities: the heritages of scientism, objectivism, and instrumentalism, though largely invisible and normalized, stand between us and genuinely *good* science.

1 | *Scientism*

Scientism is roughly coeval with science,[1] but the two should not be confused. Scientism is the assumption that "only scientific knowledge counts as real knowledge" (Williams, 2015, p. 6), but this is not an assumption inherent to science, nor one that all scientists make. In fact, there is no one thing that could be called science and so no coherent, unified object that could stand for the totality of objective truth. Though science is often cast (particularly by those of a scientistic bent) as a single, unified "method" or approach, scientists have actually worked under quite variable assumptions. As Paul Feyerabend (1993) points out in *Against Method*, there is no definition of science that includes everything we call science while excluding everything we do not. Science is too complex, spans too much history, embodies too much cultural and human variability to be understood in terms of one fully consistent set of assumptions or practices.

Accordingly, a scientific exceptionalism privileging "the methods and assumptions underlying the natural sciences" (Williams, 2015, p. 6) is basically nonsense because "there is no one 'scientific method'" (Feyerabend, 1987, p. 36). Science as actually practiced has involved a tremendous variability of method, across time (compare Roger Bacon and James Watson), discipline (compare Harry Harlow and Jane Goodall), and place (compare Wilhelm Wundt and John Watson). Science is not a method but a history and a culture, "a network of material practices, built environments (laboratories, instrumentation, etc.), traditions of apprenticeship, and learned rituals that emerged over time, in particular configurations, in different places" (Smith, 2015, p. 181).

Science has been, and is, many (sometimes contradictory) things and scientism is thus a misreading of the nature and limits of science, a kind of science boosterism that ignores the complexities of history. That

---

[1] Even Galileo had an exaggerated confidence in what science could do.

boosterism includes both "extend[ing] the natural sciences beyond their proper sphere of explanatory competence" (Hacker, 2015, p. 97) as well as encouraging "an exaggerated confidence in science (i.e., natural science in all its avatars) to produce knowledge and solve the problems facing humanity" (Williams, 2015, pp. 6–7).

Scientism, in short, is an "idolatry of scientific method" (Gadamer, 1975b, p. 316), and so is probably best understood as "a kind of fundamentalism" (Principe, 2015, p. 51). Under a fundamentalist account, the assumptions that frame a given institution are not subject to criticism or even discussion: "to the fundamentalist it is not just that the question of interpretation does not arise, the very idea is anathema, a heresy, a snare, a delusion" (van Fraasen, 2015, p. 81). Science understood as epistemically privileged invokes precisely this kind of immunity to critique or interpretation – under scientism, science makes a claim on truth that cannot be legitimately challenged by any other form or tradition of knowing.

The trouble with this sort of dogmatism is not just that it "fetters thought as cruelly as ever the churches had done" (Polanyi, 1958, p. 279), but that when we take it into our bodies, we also increase our immunity to certain kinds of critique. Under scientism, legitimacy comes in being a science and this means distancing our methods from those of philosophy, history, the humanities, and other humanizing and contextualizing traditions. Scientism can thus breed in us an unwillingness to accept limitations or take correction in the service of human or moral concerns. A basic scientistic assumption is that, on matters of truth, the facts decide, and science grants a special access to those facts; other considerations (other forms of wisdom, other obligations, other desires) can step to the back of the line.[2] Scientism thus inoculates us against the ways of knowing that reveal to us our human, moral, cultural, social, and historical contexts and attendant responsibilities.

At this point, it should be obvious that scientism is a term of abuse rather than anything someone might claim for herself; it is an *accusation*. But is it a fair one? Do any scientists really understand their work in this way? Or, more specific to my purposes here, do any psychologists understand their work in this way? The simple answer, of course, is that some do and some do not, but not in equal

---

[2] Or maybe just get in a different, much less important, line.

proportions. Though there is no way to fully document the degree to which scientism is represented in psychology, the available evidence suggests that it is the predominant view.

Sigmund Koch, who oversaw the monumental mid-century self-evaluation *Psychology: A Study of a Science*, certainly saw scientism as the mainstream view. Writing in 1981, he decried the "restrictive scientism and rule-saturated ideologies of the psychological and social sciences" (p. 82), seeing in them and their pretense to "preemptive truths," a "grave moral issue reflective of a widespread moral bankruptcy within psychology" (p. 93). Koch (1973) attributed psychology's scientism to a sort of wish-fulfillment fantasy, where the "entire ... history of psychology can be seen as a ritualistic endeavor to emulate the forms of science in order to sustain the delusion that it already is a science" (p. 636). This desire has taken form, according to Koch (1981), as "a loose melange of vaguely apprehended ideas derived from logical positivism, operationism, and neopragmatism" (p. 81); a never-renounced positivist allegiance to "philosophies of science that had begun to crumble even before psychologists borrowed their authority and that are now seen as shallow and defective by all save the borrowers" (pp. 80–81).

Koch's critique is unforgiving (and perhaps somewhat overdrawn) but not unusual. Countless historians and scholars (e.g., Kurt Danziger, Kenneth Gergen, Richard Williams, Jill Morawski, among many others) have made closely related arguments. We should, of course, be careful about relying too much on critical accounts, but the notion that psychology is scientistic is not particularly controversial, nor hard to accredit. Scientistic claims can be found everywhere in in the discipline, usually without apology or caveat.

For example, in an analysis I conducted of commonly used methods texts (Clegg, 2016), the picture of psychology that emerged was uniformly scientistic. In these texts, science was characterized as "a framework for drawing on independent realities to evaluate claims rather than to depend on tradition, authority, or armchair reasoning" (Rosnow and Rosenthal, 2008, p. 6) and psychology as one of its success stories: "the one hundred or so years in which people have conducted systematic research on human behavior have taught us more than we learned in the hundreds of centuries that preceded the last one hundred years" (Pelham and Blanton, 2007, p. 4).

This sort of scientistic vision can also be seen in disciplinary and professional documents. For example, the *APA Presidential Task Force on Evidence-Based Practice* (2006) includes a clear statement of epistemic privilege: "the scientific method is a way of thinking and observing systematically, and it is the best tool we have for learning about what works for whom" (p. 280). Similarly, in the *Report of the American Psychological Association 2009 Presidential Task Force on the Future of Psychology as a STEM Discipline* (2010), science is described as the "foundation of teaching, research, and practice in psychology" (p. 13) and psychological science as "a form of engineering" (p. 9) that plays a "critical role ... in solving society's problems" (p. 16). That report makes other fairly typical scientistic arguments for psychology's status as a science, including the claim that psychology "has used state-of-the-art scientific instrumentation since its inception" (p. 7) and that "psychological researchers routinely use sophisticated mathematics" (p. 8) as well as "experiments to gain basic knowledge" (p. 8).[3]

This sort of scientism remains largely invisible and normalized, but it is sometimes made explicit. A particularly dramatic example is the 2016 *American Psychologist* article where Timothy Melchert makes the rather startling claim that "psychology is no longer a preparadigmatic academic discipline, but has become one of the paradigmatic natural sciences" (p. 490). According to Melchert, this assertion is "fully accepted across the behavioral sciences generally" (p. 489)[4] and for this reason it "might be considered irresponsible for [professional practice] not to systematically transition to the new scientific framework" (pp. 494–495). Melchert vaguely ties this new framework to evolutionary theory and to "the invention and use of more powerful and precise scientific tools" (p. 490), claiming that "there is now overwhelming evidence supporting this perspective" (p. 491). His conclusion is that theoretical debate is essentially ended: "from a paradigmatic scientific perspective, one does not select from an array of competing theoretical orientations or philosophies for

---

[3] Common enough arguments, even though many scientists do not routinely employ sophisticated mathematics, instruments, or experiments.

[4] A claim that couldn't possibly be substantiated but that seems implausible, given the difficulty of getting any two psychologists to agree about anything.

understanding natural phenomena" but instead theories are "tested and verified using experimental research methods" (p. 491).[5]

Ignoring for the moment the fact that basically none of these assertions is actually true (and that most couldn't even be shown to be true),[6] these claims are beautifully paradigmatic of scientism. Melchert does not make any attempt to describe the complexities and nuances of scientific research as actually practiced in psychology but, instead, provides sweeping generalizations about a scientific psychology that can no longer be legitimately challenged.

And this broad rejection of anything outside the bounds of science (variously conceived) is really the point of the scientistic critique. A critique of scientism is a critique of exceptionalism, of privilege. Science is a vitally, indispensably, important human institution – one of the most important in history – but this cannot justify an immunity to critique or an arrogant dismissiveness of complexity, dissent, or alternative perspectives. If I can avoid reflection, engagement with different viewpoints, or social or moral critique simply by claiming the label "science," then only dogmatism and fiat can result; this is always the result of unchecked fundamentalism. That kind of hubris is the enemy of good, responsible science.

---

[5] It is not clear how Melchert thinks we can test theories or run experiments without a theoretical orientation.

[6] There is certainly not one unified view of science in psychology; there would be no way to show that every scientific psychologist agreed about any given claim or perspective; there is no definitive way to "show" that a discipline is paradigmatic science, and so on.

2 | *Objectivism*

Just as in scientism, where "good science is turned into bad, because barren, ideology" (Feyerabend, 1987, p. 38), in objectivism, sensible practices are overgeneralized into bad philosophy; bad, not just because objectivism is not a fully coherent philosophical position but because it entails dangerous moral consequences. Just as scientism foments immunity to critique, objectivism obscures privilege and undermines our sense of relational responsibility.

The philosophy of objectivism, which is basically the requirement that all genuine ("true" or "truth-like") knowledge be observer-independent, is quite distinct from scientific practices aimed at producing objectivity, and so some clarification is in order. Clarity can be particularly difficult in this case, as the meanings and uses of objectivity vary substantially across time and context. In fact, at one time, the terms "objectivity" and "subjectivity" "meant almost precisely the opposite of what they mean today" (Daston and Galison, 2007, p. 29). Criteria for objectivity have included "emotional detachment in one case; automatic procedures for registering data in another; recourse to quantification in still another; belief in a bedrock reality independent of human observers in yet another" (p. 29).

Still, contemporary (and most historical) writing in and about science seems to fairly consistently move between two closely related notions of objectivity – what Daston and Galison (2007) call mechanical objectivity and structural objectivity. Those who strive for mechanical objectivity take the vagaries of individual interpretation to be destructive of consistent observation and attempt to mitigate these through "self-denial coupled with the drive toward disciplined automaticity" (p. 179). From this point of view, science becomes "the fruit of good method, not of good men" and "the methods of science ... like machines that any man might own and use" (Proctor, 1991, pp. 26–27). The intended (and often actual) result of this mechanized approach to the recording of observations is greater consistency in observations recorded across time, person, and context.

Structural objectivity is also counterposed against the idiosyncrasies of individual interpretation but concerns the transmission, rather than the recording, of observations. Structurally objective knowledge is composed only of those "aspects of scientific knowledge that survive translation, transmission, theory change, and differences among thinking beings due to physiology, psychology, history, culture, language, and . . . species" (Daston and Galison, 2007, p. 256). The "techniques" of structural objectivity are those that allow the construction of abstracted accounts; accounts that, as much as possible, remain "invariant under changes of perspective" (p. 304) and so can travel between different interpretive and predictive contexts.

It is not difficult to see how the techniques of structural and mechanical objectivity could be tremendously important for the everyday practice of science. Mechanized observation procedures (including standardized techniques and equipment) ensure more uniform recordings across the highly variable contexts of scientific observation, and a shared abstract language permits a fairly standard communication, coordination, and (under the best of circumstances) extrapolation of interpretations. The techniques of objectivity are a social and technical machinery for the production of consistency, a quality indispensable to science.

Not just science, but likely any complex and distributed technical activity will make use of these techniques. In musical composition, for example, the highly variable and idiosyncratic interpretations of a given musical performance can be abstracted to a standard uniform notation that can be interpreted consistently enough to produce comparable performances across time, performer, and venue. The consistency of these performances can be increased through various techniques and equipment – tempo can be regulated through practices such as conducting or machinery such as a metronome; interpretation can be made more standard through notations on dynamics or through performance notes; and performance in general can be made more consistent through replication (i.e., "practice"). These practices are as much forms of mechanical and structural objectivity as are the comparable "bench" techniques in science.

So, in science and out, the techniques of objectivity are useful for producing consistency. Where, then, is the trouble? As long as we understand these practices heuristically – that is, as useful in the creation of consistency but not necessarily useful for (and maybe even detrimental to) other important ends – then I don't see that there is much trouble. Precision and consistency help us play together, but interpretation, improvisation, experimentation, mutual response, and adaptation, these are how we actually make music. Every performer (and composer) knows that musical notations are a guide, a heuristic, but that only gifted and trained performers can supply all that is required to make these into music.

Likewise, the technical procedures and languages of science are heuristic guides – or "maxims," to use Polanyi's (1958) term – but only the experienced, morally engaged scientist can appropriately apply and interpret these, adapt them to circumstances, and make the moral determinations, imaginative leaps, and so on that will turn these into good practice and meaningful knowledge. Thus, rigidly procedur-alizing scientific techniques and languages into the normative epistemology of objectivism – or, in Maslow's (1966) words, "to get pious and metaphysical about these personal preferences and to exalt them into rules for everyone else" (p. 57) – is as destructive of scientific understanding as it would be of musical expression. An overgeneral-ization of objectivity into a universal epistemological mandate for observer-independent knowledge (i.e., objectivism) burdens us with a task both impossible and undesirable – a task something like produ-cing interpretation-free music. In what follows, I will review, in turn, both the impossibility and the undesirability of objectivism.

The Theoretical Limitations of Objectivism

From the point of view of this book, the impossibility of observer-independent knowledge is a secondary consideration, the more import-ant matters having to do with the moral consequences of objectivism. Nevertheless, it is worth pointing out, as I will do as succinctly as possible here, that even if we wanted observer-independent knowledge, we can't have it.

The very notion of observer-independent knowledge seems absurd on its face, as knowing always, and by definition, requires a knower; it is literally impossible to produce or even conceive of knowledge that does not depend upon the particular persons who know it. Of course, what is really sought in "observer-independence" is not knowledge without a knower but knowledge that will be the same for all knowers – that is, true in itself, regardless of individual interpretation. Objectivism thus rests on "the basic conviction that there is or must be some permanent, ahistorical matrix or framework to which we can ultimately appeal in determining the nature of rationality, knowledge, truth, reality, goodness, or rightness" (Bernstein, 1983, p. 8).

But even if we grant some such independent reality, our "access" to it must still pass through particular knowers in particular communities of understanding, and so observer-independence remains an essentially empty metaphysical postulate.[1] "As human beings, we must inevitably see the universe from a centre lying within ourselves and speak about it in terms of a human language shaped by the exigencies of human intercourse. Any attempt rigorously to eliminate our human perspective from our picture of the world must lead to absurdity" (Polanyi, 1958, p. 2). The best we can do is work from those paradigms and theories that produce the most consistent observations across person, time, and context.

But this may be good enough. In science, we don't need definitive proofs but continual, collective, and fallibilist approximations of the best accounts possible. This is more or less the vision that Popper, and later Lakatos, imagined for science, and seems to be the one most current in psychology (see Clegg, 2016). On this account, objectivism is less about warranting independent foundations for absolutely true knowledge, and more about mitigating the idiosyncrasies of interpretation (i.e., "biases") inherent to human activity; about "the immunization of the cognitive from the normative" (Smith, 1993, p. 7) through a system of collective checks and standardized procedures.

I think we all know this account pretty well: science draws its moral authority from this notion that the conclusions of science can achieve, or at least approach, a neutral representation of the facts, cleansed of individual bias through objectivist practices. Unfortunately, however, the notion of neutrality is at least as suspect as the notion of observer-independence:

It is now widely recognized that science serves certain interests, that science is rarely neutral insofar as it touches the vital affairs of humanity – our health,

---

[1] This is more or less where Kant left the matter, postulating a noumenal realm constituting an unknowable foundation for a phenomenal reality that we can know.

our status, our wealth and power, our security, our happiness – that science is not neutral in regard to these things but participates in their fulfillment or frustration. (Proctor, 1991, p. 224)

Scientists, and thus science, cannot be neutral, and thus "the ideal of objectivity as neutrality is widely regarded to have failed not only in history and the social sciences, but also in philosophy and related fields such as jurisprudence" (Harding, 1992, pp. 569–570).

Neutrality as a scientific criterion fails not just because a particular scientist must always have a perspective and can never be personally neutral but because even the so-called self-correcting systems and procedures of science are themselves woven from particular value-orientations. Helen Longino (1995) has made this point quite effect-ively in her analysis of the epistemic values (empirical adequacy, parsi-mony, etc.) generally considered foundational to science. Her analysis suggests that all epistemic values "import significant socio-political values" into science and that "even the apparently neutral criteria of accuracy or empirical adequacy can involve socio-political dimensions in the judgment of *which* data a theory or model must agree with" (p. 396). Kitcher (2003)[2] comes to a similar conclusion, arguing that, in science, "the questions we pose, the apparatus we employ, the categories that frame our investigations, even the objects we probe, are as they are because of the moral, social, and political ideals of our predecessors" (p. 86) and so "moral and social values [are] intrinsic to the practice of the sciences" (p. 65).

The value-ladenness of even basic scientific decisions (such as those concerning the adequacy of evidence) is seen, by many philosophers, sociologists, and historians of science, as incorrigible, in large part because of what is generally referred to as the underdetermination of theory by data. Underdetermination holds that "since any theory presupposes various background beliefs and assumptions – including norms regarding what counts as evidence – the theory makes claims that go beyond what can be established by observational evidence alone" (Padovani, Richardson, and Tsou, 2015, p. 4). Moreover, there

---

[2] It is worth noting here that Longino and Kitcher represent a move among analytic, and particularly Anglo-American, philosophers of science toward a more contextualist account of science, as opposed to the strictly empiricist accounts that psychology imported in the mid-twentieth century (and that still inform most thinking about science in psychology).

is, in principle, always more than one theory or interpretation consistent with a given set of facts, and there is also always the possibility that future facts will disconfirm present theory. Thus, theory choice and theory revision can never be based on purely empirical considerations and will always depend to some degree on extra-empirical considerations, including social, moral, and political commitments.

Feyerabend (1987) puts the matter succinctly: "questions of fact and reality depend on questions of value" (p. 252), and method, however systematic, provides no escape from this condition. But, really, is there anything so shocking in this conclusion? "How could it be otherwise if science is done by real human beings living and working in real human communities?" (Howard, 2009, p. 203). It is hard to imagine any scientist actually being surprised by the notion that her work might not be completely value-neutral. The notion of neutrality has always functioned more as a political tool than as an actual descriptor of, or guide for, real scientific practice.

In his careful historical study of value-neutrality in science, Proctor (1991) points to the different political deployments of scientific neutrality, and their range is impressive. In seventeenth-century Europe, scientific neutrality was part of the "royalist compromise": "science needed funding and the Crown needed gunpowder. In the bargain struck, scientists received funds and social space to work (especially freedom from censorship), but traded away all rights to moral disputation and political engagement" (p. 38). Neutrality was dismissed as illusory and unpatriotic by both the Nazis and the "party" in Bolshevik Russia, while it was affirmed and deployed as a screen for eugenicist values in early twentieth-century North America and late twentieth-century South Africa. Neutrality, in short, is not so much a real attribute of science as an opportunistic rhetoric, deployed both to defend the boundaries of science – "the 'purity' of science is generally defended in the degree that its autonomy is perceived to be under siege" (p. 72) – and to obscure "the fact that science has social origins and social consequences" (p. x).

The Tyranny of Hidden Prejudices

But science does have social origins and consequences, and to obscure these, as in objectivism, is not only to subscribe to an incoherent philosophy, but it is also to isolate scientists and consumers of science from the moral affordances and obligations of science work. Objectivism isolates us from our moral obligations, first, because its practices obscure inequality and so privilege power, and, second, because these practices intentionally dehumanize (or, perhaps, devalorize) and can thus anesthetize us against our sense of relational responsibility.

Objectivism obscures inequality because it obscures the whole range of prejudices encoded into normalized scientific practices. If neutrality and observer-independence fail as meaningful criteria, then our persistence in these becomes performative and so obscures and foments, rather than eliminates, systemic abuse and bias. In other words, objectivism does not allow us to *be* less biased, but to *appear* less biased, and this constitutes a perfect cover for biases and abuses of all kinds. This is why Gadamer refers to objectivism as a "tyranny of hidden prejudices" (Gadamer, 1975b, p. 272).

This tyranny can be hidden in individual bias but is really more pernicious in systemic biases, a point that feminist and other critical theorists have been making for a very long time now. Proctor (1991) gives the example of turn-of-the-century German sociologists, for whom "the ideal of neutrality (or objectivity) was defined in such a way as to exclude women from science," their explicit assumption being that "women cannot achieve the distance or detachment from objects necessary to pursue objective science" (p. 117). General prejudices of this kind dominate entire fields and hide particular interests and systemic inequalities behind "a mask, disguising whatever interests may lie behind the origins and maintenance of research priorities" (p. 230). The rhetorics of objectivism and neutrality thus raise a "fog of war" behind which various hidden interests or inequalities may operate, and this will be true even without (especially without) any particular acknowledged agenda.

Thus, the pretense of value-independence prevents us from a real engagement with the contradictions, inequalities, divided allegiances, and so on that structure our disciplines, and so objectivism does not just obscure bias but privileges power. This is true, in part, because "social science usually, readily, and uncritically serves the interests of those who pay for it" (Haan, Bellah, Rabinow, and Sullivan, 1983, p. 5), and so "an uncritical pursuit of social scientific knowledge will almost certainly work to reinforce the existing powers in society that fund that research" (p. 4). But this privileging of power also occurs because long-standing inequalities structure the assumptions, languages, practices, and institutions of science. Sandra Harding (1992) has provided a nuanced critique of this dynamic, arguing that when systemic prejudices dominate a particular scientific community, "power is exercised ... through the dominant institutional structures, priorities, practices, and languages of the sciences" (p. 567). She refers to this as a "'depoliticization' of science" that freezes critique and dissent, normalizing the existing power structures as a kind of "authoritarian science" (pp. 567–568).

According to Harding (1992), this authoritarian science has been principally shaped by "the institutionalized, normalized politics of male supremacy, class exploitation, racism, and imperialism" that "'depoliticize' Western scientific institutions and practices, thereby shaping our images of the natural and social worlds and legitimating past and future exploitative public policies" (p. 568). Under these conditions,

the neutrality ideal provides no resistance to the production of systematically distorted results of research. Even worse, it defends and legitimates the institutions and practices through which the distortions and their exploitative consequences are generated. It certifies as value-neutral, normal, natural, and therefore not political at all the existing scientific policies and practices through which powerful groups can gain the information and explanations that they need to advance their priorities. (p. 568)

This inequality is made unassailable through a pretense of neutrality that "defines the objections of its victims and any criticisms of its institutions, practices, or conceptual world as agitation by special interests that threatens to damage the neutrality of science. Thus, when sciences are already in the service of the mighty, scientific neutrality ensures that 'might makes right'" (p. 569).

In the case of "the androcentric, Eurocentric, and racist assumptions in many of the most widely accepted scientific claims" (Harding, 1992, p. 574), Harding's case is not difficult to accredit. There is no question that scientists have severely misrepresented and misused women and colonized peoples,[3] and this is hardly surprising. Obviously, "discriminatory and less than maximally reliable results [from] research that supported inequity were the logical outcome of sciences

---

[3] Among others, including those labeled "disabled," those in the LGBTQ community, and pretty nearly all oppressed or marginalized groups.

designed by societies invested in inequity" (p. 44). Rather than protecting science from such powerful interests, objectivism, and the illusion of neutrality, have long served as the perfect vehicles for the institutionalization of privilege.

The Moral Anesthetic of Objectivism

The privileging of power is the more public and structural face of objectivism, but there is an equally destructive relational dynamic at the heart of objectivist practice. I refer to the anesthetizing force of a practice that takes dehumanization as its avowed purpose. Under objectivism,[4] "inquiring action is so rigidly and fully regulated by rule," often "the rules totally displace their human users" (Koch, 1981, p. 79). Under these conditions, "objects of knowledge become caricatures, if not faceless, and thus they lose reality. The world, or any given part of it, is not felt fully or passionately" (p. 79), and scientific observation comes to "register its object as faceless, undifferentiated, psychically distant – to be, so to say, cognitively anesthetic" (p. 79).

Maslow (1966) warned of this relational anesthetic when he suggested that a scientist attempting to be objectivist "may feel it necessary to drown his human feelings for the people he studies" (p. 116). Joseph Gluck (2016), a former animal researcher, offers a very lucid description of how objectivism can function in this anesthetic way. He recounts struggling with the horrors often involved in animal research and the conflict between his personal responses and the dispassionate and distancing rhetorics of objectivism: "I came to see that my natural recoil from intentionally harming animals was a hindrance to how I understood scientific progress" (para. 4). He deployed various justifications for his part in this work, such as reassuring himself that he was "being responsible by providing good nutrition, safe cages, skilled and caring caretakers and veterinarians for the animals," and this "made [his] transition to a more 'rigorous' stance easier than [he] could have imagined" (para. 5). Even from this "rigorous stance," however, he found it "impossible to fully quell [his] repugnance at all that [he] continued to witness and to inflict" (para. 7).

---

[4] Which Sigmund Koch sometimes, as in the following quote, refers to as "ameaningful thinking."

What is most telling in this account is that as objectivist practice required harm, it also required a kind of strategic violence to spontaneous feelings of responsibility and to the sense of repugnance at violence to another living creature. Gluck felt the need to quell his pity and mercy. Objectivist laboratory practices and discourses allow researchers to insulate themselves from such feelings, and objectivist publishing practices do the same for consumers via reports that are "sanitized, stripped of descriptive language, deliberately preventing the reader from getting a true picture of the emotional and physical torment inherent in the research" (para. 9).

In practice, then, objectivism often requires an intentional maiming of our moral responsiveness. We might call this "impartiality," but sometimes what this really means is that we are suppressing those parts of ourselves that cherish and protect others, leaving them to the mercy of whatever mercenary motives remain. Gluck highlights the consequences of this moral self-harm when he describes his former perception of a lab animal as "just an animated object that produced data points" (para. 7) and his incredulity when a graduate student wished "to dedicate his doctoral dissertation to G44, a female rhesus monkey who had unexpectedly died during his research" (para. 7).

The moral costs of objectivism are easier to see in cases like these, where researchers can know that they are doing harm and still feel justified. But these moral costs accrue even when they are not so dramatically visible. Those who study science have, repeatedly and for centuries, warned that "attempts to treat man as an object or a thing are potentially dangerous, dehumanizing, and insidious" (Rabinow, 1983, p. 52) and that "a procedure whose main aim it is to get rid of all human elements is bound to lead to inhuman actions" (Feyerabend, 1987, p. 299). They have also warned of a world devalorized (Koyre's term) and disenchanted (Weber's term), "stripped of its qualities, of teleology, of magical resonances and meanings" (Proctor, 1991, p. 7). Maslow (1966) called this "the desacralizing of science, the banishment of all the experiences of transcendence from the realm of the respectably known and the respectably knowable, and the denial of a systematic place in science for awe, wonder, mystery, ecstasy, beauty, and peak experiences" (p. 121). He feared that under objectivism, science could come to be seen as "a contaminator, a spoiler, a reducer, that makes life bleak and mechanical, robs it of color and joy, and imposes on it a spurious certainty" (p. 138).

Maslow had a deep respect, even love, for science and wanted to save it from this fate. Polanyi (1958) felt much the same, warning that "a philosophic movement guided by aspirations of scientific severity has come to threaten the position of science itself" (p. 150). Objectivism, for Polanyi, endangers science, because "a passion for achieving absolutely impersonal knowledge" leaves us "unable to recognize any persons" and "presents us with a picture of the universe in which we ourselves are absent. In such a universe there is no one capable of creating and upholding scientific values; hence there is no science" (p. 150).

3 | *Instrumentalism*

My argument so far has been that, like scientism, objectivism places scientists in a false and compromised position; makes unfulfillable promises, in the process creating a technology of obfuscation that not only hides privilege and inequity, but can cloud and compromise moral judgment. Yet, despite these critiques, one might ask whether any of this matters so long as science works.[1] Perhaps objectivism is not fully coherent as a philosophical position and perhaps it even carries some troubling moral consequences, but would the tremendous progress of science be possible without it and would anyone wish to give away a tradition of practice so spectacularly successful?

What is hidden in an otherwise admirably pragmatic focus on "what works" is the real subject of the sentence (and, indeed, of science) – that is, "for whom" science works. What "works" (or what is "successful" or is "progress") is determined by one's projects and values and so when I make an appeal to a pragmatic view of science, I am really making a tacit avowal that current scientific practice "works" for *me*. Of course, no one is likely to make the argument that way, exactly – no one says, "the objectivist and exceptionalist view of science seems to be serving my privilege just fine, so I don't see any reason to question it." Instead, we might say something seemingly uncontroversial like "science is neutral and its products serve everyone equally."

But science has not always served, and almost certainly never will serve, everyone equally. As long as science lives in unequal societies, those inequalities will live in science:

The categories in terms of which we describe nature are responses to human interests, and, when inquiry is dominated by the interests of a particular group, there may be alternative classifications, alternative practices, and

---

[1] It got us to the moon, dammit!

29

alternative modifications of the world that might have suited a broader range of human concerns. (Kitcher, 2003, p. 175)

Thus, to take an instrumental view of science – that is, to cast scientific findings as neutral and to justify scientist actions purely (or primarily) in terms of their pragmatic utility – is to ignore whatever inequity, harm, or oppression lies within the chosen emphases and sanctioned norms of current scientific practice. The instrumental view of science – the focus on "what works" – is a tacit acceptance of the status quo and of whatever injustice or harm that may inscribe. I have already alluded to the many ways that science has encoded and enacted various forms of injustice, but a slightly more specific accounting of these in psychology will help clarify the dangers of an instrumental approach to science.

Instrumentalism in the History of Psychology

Psychology's history seems to suggest that "instrumental" is the right descriptor for our discipline's general moral tenor. From the early days of the discipline, psychologists[2] have understood their role as helping "to administer the masses effectively" (Walsh, 2015, p. 97). The vast majority of all psychological research has been funded by large institutions – military, medical, corporate, academic, philanthropic, and so on – and the products of that research have, not coincidentally, been tools of adaptation to the existing environment (i.e., to the status quo). Psychologists have produced the assessments that accredit persons by their adequate performance in schools, governments, and corporations, by their skills and capacities to contribute to civil society, by their mental and emotional fitness for the exercise of liberty, and so on, and psychologists have built the concepts, tools, and infrastructures to modify those persons (or behaviors) not fit for, not adapting to, those institutional structures. Psychologists have thus primarily functioned "as 'architects of adjustment' in preserving the status quo" (Sugarman, 2015, p. 115) and their work as a kind of "social engineering to ensure that citizens adapted to their station in life" (Walsh, 2015, p. 97). Walsh (2015) puts it rather boldly: "psychology has been and remains an administrative tool for society's power brokers, that is, our activities have and continue to enhance the efficacy

---

[2] Particularly North Americans, but really psychologists of all stripes.

of society's economic, educational, and governmental institutions" (p. 96).

Psychology understood instrumentally – that is, in terms of what "works" within the status quo – thus provides a very clear answer to the question of "for whom" psychology (or science) works: whoever pays for it. Or, more precisely, an instrumentalist psychology "works" for those with the influence and resources to support, commission, and deploy research. When we turn our attention to those for whom psychology has not always worked (those who have not had the influence or resources to command it), the abuses, harms, and injustices of psychological research become clear.

Nonhuman animals, for example, are probably the "participants" in psychology with the least power, and their lot has been, and remains, correspondingly gruesome. Most readers will have likely heard of the most famous cases of animal cruelty in psychological research. In his study of unique facial expressions, for example, Carney Landis required subjects to behead live rats (the beheading performed for them if they refused). Harry Harlow's research with rhesus monkeys (Blum, 1996) involved raising infant monkeys in isolation for as much as a year, subjecting them to sensory deprivation in what he called the "pit of despair" (leading to very disturbed behavior), and the use of a device he called the "rape rack," which involved restraining disturbed female monkeys so that these could be forcibly impregnated by male monkeys. In 1969, Deneau, Yanagita, and Seevers catheterized monkeys so that they could self-administer cocaine and other addictive drugs; during the trials, monkeys developed extremely disturbed behavior (confusion, hallucinations, biting and scratching themselves, tearing off their own fingers, plucking out all of their hair) and severe physical complications (seizures, rapid weight loss, and usually death).

These cases are famous for various reasons, but they are by no means unprecedented. The history of psychological research on animals involves countless examples of physically and psychologically cruel and destructive actions, and these continue. Research involving protocols similar to (and inspired by) Harlow's work continued, as recently as 2014, at the University of Wisconsin (Phillips, 2014) and at the NIH (Kraft, 2015). Addiction studies in animals similar to the 1969 monkey studies have proliferated (Banks, Czoty, and Negus, 2017). And, generally, animal research in psychology routinely involves dismemberment, disfiguration, confinement, and isolation.

Regardless of whether one feels inclined to offer instrumental justifications for this work, there is no question that harm, and the willingness to inflict harm, are inseparable from it.

This pattern of harm being exported to those least able to resist is the standard one under the instrumentalist moral logic of scientific research. The most extreme cases involving humans are those associated with oppressive regimes or organizations subjecting subordinate groups ("criminals," homosexuals, racial minorities, the poor, the "disabled," etc.) to research without their consent – the human experimentation, for example, in Nazi Germany, Stalinist Russia, and Imperial Japan, military experimentation in the USA, South Africa, and elsewhere, research in hospitals, orphanages, and other "social service" institutions, and so on. There is a long tradition of using subaltern groups (so-called "vulnerable populations") for research in psychology (and out). Perhaps the most famous case in psychology is the "Little Albert" experiment, where Watson and Rayner "borrowed" a child from an orphanage in order to condition fear responses in the infant. Psychologists in South Africa (some of whom continue as active professionals in good standing) also famously exploited an oppressed group, forcing gay members of the security forces to undergo aversion therapy, chemical castration, and forced sex-change operations. Psychologists working within the US military chain of command participated in, observed, advised on, and helped to legitimate the torture of prisoners (mostly of Middle Eastern descent).[3] And, of course, the history of treatment of (including research on) institutionalized persons could produce its own litany of harms.

Many more examples of specific harm administered to marginalized classes could follow. But the larger point is that these harms nearly always occur as part of the sanctioned practices of psychology and this is unsurprising given that, in essentially all cases, the harm (and the research) is performed *by* those in socially privileged circumstances and *on* those in socially underprivileged circumstances. In other words, the instrumentalist approach to science has sanctioned, as Melba Vasquez (2012) said in her APA presidential address, "the abuse of psychological science to support and maintain destructive, and at times

---

[3] "Psychologists participated in waterboarding and in other enhanced techniques that may or may not include hooding, wall standing, subjecting to noise, deprivation of sleep, stress positions, sensory deprivation, cold cells, and isolation" (Teo, 2015, p. 82).

horrific and gruesome, practices to maintain the status quo of domin-
ance and subordination" (p. 337).

But these specific cases of harm are only a part of the story. Much
broader kinds of harm are attributable to psychology, not through
particular cases of abuse, but through more general contributions to
various forms of injustice or oppression. As Teo (2015) argues,

> Throughout its history empirical psychology has produced research that
> must be labeled as racist, classist, and sexist (Teo, 2014). Empirical methods
> and verbal commitments to "objectivity" have not prevented the reality that
> racialized minorities, women, gays and lesbians, subaltern groups, people
> living in poverty, and people with disabilities have been constructed as
> inferior or problematic. (p. 79)

This construction of marginalized groups as lesser, damaged, or "disordered" has taken many forms through psychology's history (and
I can only give them a shallow gloss here). Racial minority groups,
for example, have been cast as "degenerate" in various ways – explicitly through eugenic theories, procedurally through the mass administration of intelligence testing, functionally through disease or
dysfunction classifications like "protest psychosis" (Bromberg and
Simon, 1968), structurally through participation in racist political
practices like the "stolen generations" in Australia or mass incarceration in the USA, and so on. Women have been cast as "disordered" in
similar ways, through explicitly misogynist theories that cast women as
"hysterical,"[4] irrational, overly emotional, and so on, through various
forms of research or testing showing gendered "differences" then
interpreted as inferiorities, through participation in oppressive political
practices (supporting the restriction of women to traditional roles,
supporting denying them the vote or property ownership, etc.), and
so on. This is a common pattern in the history of psychology: (some)[5]
psychologists provide rationales for the oppression of politically marginal groups on the basis of their inferior qualities or dispositions and

---

[4] From the Greek *hystera*, or "womb."
[5] My focus here is on ways that psychologists have contributed to harm or
injustice, so these are highlighted, but there is tremendous variability among
psychologists, and no description here is intended to apply to all. Many
psychologists have advocated women's rights, animal rights, and other reforms to
unjust or exploitative practices.

these are encoded in "objective" categories like intelligence or mental health. This same pattern has been followed closely with immigrants, the "disabled," members of the LGBTQ community (homosexuality remaining a "disease" in the DSM until the late 1970s), and so on.

The Point

I dwell on these larger examples of psychologist complicity in injustice because they highlight the fact that the problems I am pointing to here are systemic rather than individual; these cases are general and emblematic (though obviously far from universal) rather than examples of rogue psychologists operating outside the bounds of disciplinary sanction. Scientific psychology, imagined as scientistic (epistemically privileged), objectivist (neutral and independent), and instrumentalist (purely technical and practical), far from preventing such abuses, constitutes fertile soil for them. When the scientist can imagine himself as immune to any but scientific critique, as independent of political or social concerns, as just a technician focused only on what works, then he doesn't have to ask himself some difficult moral questions. He doesn't have to look for or attempt to mitigate his tendencies to privilege the status quo; he doesn't have to face the moral weight of his choices that harm those who cannot protect themselves. Scientism, objectivism, instrumentalism; these are absolution for our roles in perpetuating injustice. Even more, they are a technology for insulating ourselves from our own moral sense and moral obligations and from the hard truth that our work is often institutionalized in ways that encourage us to fail in those obligations.

Allow me to dwell for a moment on one more example that shows this point as clearly as I know how. I think most people recognize now the moral repugnance of eugenics, but in the first part of the twentieth century, a broadly eugenic outlook was a very common, even respectable, position among academics, including many eminent psychologists. Eugenic assumptions were intimately tied up in methods, particularly Galtonian approaches to statistics, in theories of personality, mental health, and development, in political practices like mass testing (as part of US immigration, military entrance exams, etc.), population control, professional practices (e.g., various forms of segregation in academia), and so on. Put simply, it was a perfectly acceptable position within scientific psychology to cast certain races (particularly "African"), classes (the "poor"), and types ("degenerate," "idiot," etc.) as genetically inferior and to propose and enact social policies designed to restrict or reduce procreation (and migration) among such groups – that is, to "improve the human stock."

Nothing about the received view of science (what I have characterized here in terms of scientism, objectivism, and instrumentalism) disqualified a eugenic approach. The work of Henry E. Garrett is a good example of this point. Garrett was a particularly eminent psychologist, serving as president of the APA in 1946 and the EPA in 1944, as the chair of the Columbia Psychology Department from 1941 to 1955, and as a member of the National Research Council. He was also notorious for conducting research to show the intellectual inferiority of "Negroes" and for his tireless advocacy for segregation (see Winston, 1998). He was an explicit eugenicist but saw this not as a moral or political commitment but as the only position consistent with the scientific evidence. He insisted that the science showed racial inferiority among blacks, and warned that "racial amalgamation would mean a general lowering of the cultural and intellectual level of the American people" (as cited in Winston, 1998, p. 183). Garrett consistently invoked the norms of scientific objectivity and accused those who opposed him of ignoring or twisting the facts.

Of course, Garrett's position was not unique and, indeed, still periodically resurfaces.[6] The same congruence between sanctioned views of scientific psychology and eugenic and racist practices was visible in South Africa during apartheid. In the early years of apartheid, psychologist complicity with apartheid was quite explicit – for example, the Carnegie Commission, many of whose members were psychologists, focused funds on exclusively white problems and, in its report, proposed penalties for sexual intercourse between the races and policies to prevent blacks from competing with whites for work (Nicholas, 2014). One of the chief architects of apartheid, Premier H. F. Verwoerd, himself held a PhD in psychology and there is some evidence that, under his administration, psychologists were contracted by the state to

---

[6] in North America, for example, in Jensen (1969), Herrnstein and Murray (1994), and Rushton (1995) (see Teo, 2015).

perform coercive interrogations, including torture (Magwaza, 2001). Even as late as 1967, P. M. Robbertse, the president of the Psychological Institute of the Republic of South Africa, made an appeal in support of segregationist research (Hook, Kiguwa, and Mkhize, 2004). In later years, psychologist complicity was more subtle, taking the form of segregated and white-dominated professional associations, a conspicuous silence in research publications on all matters of black experiences under apartheid (Seedat, 1998), and the creation and use of segregated and discriminatory systems of mental health diagnosis, training, and treatment (Magwaza, 2001).

While psychologist complicity in eugenics and apartheid involved many cases of direct harm, the more fundamental trouble revealed in these examples is that the entire institution of scientific psychology can be, and was, structured and mobilized to support discrimination and oppression. In these instances, the institutional and procedural character of scientific psychology allowed the whole to be co-opted by oppressive social agencies. Many researchers, in the name of neutrality and objectivity either ignored or actively supported injustice and inequality in their society. They reified that injustice within seemingly neutral social scientific categories and variables – like race differences in intelligence or mental health – and thus provided concepts and rationales for state-sponsored racism.

What is particularly instructive here is that this vast institutional complicity was not obviously inconsistent with the norms of science. Eugenic researchers, as much as anyone else, hewed to the norms of objectivity and neutrality (in fact, they often claimed to be the only ones doing so). They were doing perfectly acceptable scientific research. Far from preventing injustice, then, scientific psychology in this case was perfectly adaptable to it. Even more, an instrumental scientific ethics made this complicity in injustice nearly inevitable. All psychologists had to do was their jobs, without any particular dedication to a disruptive resistance to the status quo, for their work to continue codifying and dignifying generations of prejudice and oppression with the languages of scientific fact.

A Few More Words

A great many words and unpleasant historical episodes to say what I started with, which is that the received, common-sense view of science is inadequate to our moral obligation and that responsible science isn't possible as long as we remain sequestered within the false purity of scientism, objectivism, and instrumentalism. These incoherent philosophies prevent us from feeling and facing, from living and living up to, our responsibilities.

PART II

Good Science

What I have claimed so far is that scientism, objectivism, and instrumentalism can interfere with our ability to attend to our responsibilities as scientists. These can insulate us from critique, from our own moral perceptions and commitments, and from having to acknowledge the injustices inscribed in our hidden values. These assumptions about science are also simply distortions. Science has never been beyond or above values or politics and "scientific knowledge cannot be fully understood apart from its deployments in particular material, intellectual, and social contexts" (Longino, 2002, p. 9). If we look closely at what really happens when we do science, we will not see an algorithmic, "self-correcting" machine of context-independent discovery; we will see a delicate and unknowably complex architecture of embodied human interpretations, interpersonal commitments and negotiations, and historically specific institutional concretions.

If we want to make sense of this culture we call science and, more importantly, live in it responsibly and with a good conscience, we need a different story about what science is and how it works. The work of Part II is to trace the outlines of this alternative science story, with an emphasis on research in psychology. To do so, I draw primarily on scholarship in the history, sociology, and anthropology of science, as well as on the work of the many psychologists and philosophers who have attempted to make sense of psychological science.

By way of introduction, I'd like to dwell for a moment on a single question: *how do we know that a particular scientific claim is true?* A temptingly simple answer is to argue that a claim is true because existing empirical evidence is consistent with that claim. But this account is problematic for at least two reasons. First, as philosophers of science have argued for more than a century (and I have detailed in a previous chapter), there is always more than one possible interpretation for any given accumulation of data, and data cannot, by themselves, compel any particular conclusion regarding them. Data always "underdetermine" theory and so we can never rely solely on data to justify the truth of some claim; data need human interpreters and their interpretations will never be definitive.

Second, even if data could definitively accredit some claim, except in the very rare cases where I personally record every observation from some study, I will never know with certainty what actually occurred in any given study.[1] When I take a claim to be true, it will almost never be because I know that the data are consistent with the conclusions; it will almost always be because I trust in the systems and persons that produced a particular report. I trust that authors have reported findings accurately and honestly; I trust in the integrity and competence of a whole community of individuals on whose work any scientific report depends; I trust in the institutions (educational, governmental, disciplinary, etc.) that accredit that research; I trust in the integrity of the publishing process through which the findings are made public; I trust in a whole tradition of discourses and practices that my community takes to be reflective of "good" science (e.g., proper research design and data analysis procedures). Certainly, I sometimes attempt to verify the integrity of the systems I have trusted – for example, through peer review of various kinds (grant review, IRB review, re-analysis, etc.) – but this can only ever be a small sampling of the whole system. Trust in the competence and good faith of others (most of whom I do not know) will thus always be the primary epistemic warrant for my belief in any scientific claim.

It is therefore nonsense to talk of science[2] as "data-driven." Scientific facts are always hermeneutic – they are "driven" by fallible humans making informed judgments in the face of uncertainty – and scientific "truth" does not inhere in data, nor even in methods, but in the integrity of a complex historical and social system. So, how do I know that a particular claim is true? Of course, I don't. I trust the judgment calls of my fellow citizens, try to make the right calls in my own work, and do my part to assess, protect, and refine those elements of our shared scientific culture that I take to be essential to the truth or value of our work. Science is a community and it is only the integrity of

---

[1] And even then, the degrees of uncertainty involved in data collection beggar the imagination.
[2] Or, indeed, any human activity.

the community as a whole that makes "good" science. Good science is not "driven" by data or procedure, but by the good will and good faith of particular persons and by the integrity of the social systems that they nurture.

Accounts of science focusing purely on the mechanics of data manipulation or the characteristics of theory are thus fundamentally inadequate: "If we try to represent scientific practices with a model of knowledge drawn from midcentury analytic epistemology, that is, with an abstraction derived from a priori models and principles of argument, we will only succeed in offering a caricature" (Longino, 2002, pp. 37–38). Instead, "an adequate representation of scientific practices must situate scientists in their communities and situate those communities in the larger and partially overlapping communities of clients, funders, consumers, and citizens that sustain them" (p. 37).

In this book, I attempt to sketch the outlines of this larger social and moral geography for psychological science. When we look at that geography – really consider the choices, relationships, and institutions that constitute everyday science work – it becomes clear that the system wherein science sits is not fundamentally mechanical nor algorithmic, but human, and the kind of attention required to "justify" that system is not fundamentally technical, but moral.[3]

I will make this case, first, by looking, in Chapter 4, a little more concretely at what scientists actually do. The account I give there is based on historical, social, and philosophical studies of science, and so emphasizes everyday research practices. I try to show how science is organized around the collective construction of persuasive accounts and is framed by cultural (and political), professional, institutional, local (and interpersonal), and dispositional constraints and processes. This account situates science in its actual, rather than idealized, social contexts and so reveals science work as arbitrated within, and fundamentally shaped by, social, moral, and political considerations.

I argue, in Chapter 5, that the social and moral context of science demands a correspondingly social and moral approach to scientific justification. I suggest that justification should be understood not as the warranting of empirical claims, but as a collective and sustained

---

[3] This is not to say that justifying science does not entail technical competence; only that the notion of "technical competence" is derivative of a particular value stance and is thus one of many moral stances entailed in "good" science.

moral attention to the whole human and social architecture of a scientific community. We justify science by refining the institutions and practices of our research communities such that they reflect the shared values of those who participate in those communities. In Chapters 6 and 7, I outline two forms of practice that I argue are indispensable to this sort of scientific justification.

The first of these, outlined in Chapter 6, is an open disciplinary politics where the broadest possible range of qualified contributors have equal standing to challenge scientific claims and practices. This approach to disciplinary organization eschews dogmatic rhetorics of certainty in favor of a healthy, sustained critique, not only of scientific claims, but of those disciplinary practices that institutionalize inequality and other forms of privilege. I draw on decolonizing and feminist traditions to suggest various ways to institutionalize such an open disciplinary politics and advocate for an epistemic citizenship aimed at supporting reforms reflecting that commitment. In Chapter 7, I describe the second of these practices, a committed research praxis where scientists strive to articulate the community-level value commitments that define good science, and to evaluate the degree to which particular scientific activities and products reflect those commitments.

Across these four chapters, my aim is to work from faithful renderings of everyday scientific practice (in psychology and in science more generally) to provide a foundationally social and moral reading of what constitutes good psychological science and of how that science can be adequately justified.

4 | *What Scientists Do*

When we look closely at what scientists do, it becomes immediately clear that the primary products of scientific work are accounts. In their classic lab ethnography, Latour and Woolgar (1986)[1] famously make this point, describing a group of scientists "who spend the greatest part of their day coding, marking, altering, correcting, reading, and writing" (p. 49). Scientists, they say, are "writers and readers in the business of being convinced and convincing others" (p. 88) and laboratory activity is "the organisation of persuasion through literary inscription" (p. 88). Knorr-Cetina (1981) makes a related point, characterizing scientific activity as "the instrumental manufacture of knowledge ... which is constantly turned into credits in scientific everyday life via publication" (pp. 3–4). Knorr-Cetina also emphasizes the manufactured, fabricated quality of scientific work – like engineers, designers, artisans, or organizers, scientists must make things that work – but the uniquely scientific product is not technology nor machinery, but narrative. Certainly, science can entail design, engineering, craft, organizing, and so on, and doing these reliably is often a precondition for good science, but the specifically scientific goal of all this activity is to produce an abstractable and extendable *account* of it.

Such accounts must do all sorts of work: they must inscribe laboratory activities and give an accounting of how specific observations were produced; they must signal competence and proper adherence to disciplinary norms; they must make sense of (account for) all relevant, accredited scientific observations (including those being reported); they must build scientific consensus and help others reliably

---

[1] In this chapter, I make particular use of three lab ethnographies: Knorr-Cetina (1981); Latour and Woolgar (1986); and Peterson (2015, 2016). The first two of these are classics of the genre and are particularly detailed resources on everyday lab practices. The last is, to my knowledge, the only published lab ethnography focusing on psychological research, and thus of tremendous value in understanding lab practices in psychology.

predict future observations; they must (often implicitly) advocate for
(i.e., value or defend) particular traditions, questions, kinds of data,
theories, methods, forms of interpretation, and so on; they must per-
suade funders, institutional observers, editors, and other scientists that
both the account itself and the work it recounts are worthwhile.
Scientific accounts thus legitimate, organize, and mobilize a vast infra-
structure of resources and institutions and so must satisfy a wide range
of functions and constituents. The story of science, then, is the story of
how such accounts are made to work for these various ends and actors,
within specific dispositional, institutional, and material constraints,
and through the skilled navigation of a complex network of relational
processes and institutional structures.

Needless to say, the complexity of this social geography is daunting
and beyond any full articulation, but Science and Technology Studies
(STS)[2] scholars have done much to rough in the sketch. Speaking
generally, STS work points to the importance of various constraints
in framing how scientific work is produced. These include dispositional
constraints, like assumptions, beliefs, desires, habits, prejudices, commitments, interests, norms, traditions, and capacities (talent, experience, opportunities, etc.); institutional constraints like bureaucratic
forms, gatekeeping structures, and formal hierarchies; and material
constraints, like the limitations or possibilities entailed in specific kinds
of equipment, space, and resources, and their availability, reliability,
suitability, costs, and convenience.

STS analyses of scientific practice also highlight important relational
and institutional processes that frame scientific work, including: the
competition for resources (prestige, status, money, space, credibility,
etc.); persuasion, generally involving rhetorical work, credit- and
support-seeking, and sometimes coercion (or other less friendly strategies); the continual negotiation of commitments, resources, and institutional constraints among partnerships, group memberships, and
other kinds of alliances; the management and organization of
institutions and persons (generally involving oversight, dispute resolution, gatekeeping, and the arbitration of hierarchies, priorities, pre-
cedence, labor, etc.); and building – that is, the collective task of

---

[2] I am using STS as a shorthand term for a whole array of disciplines (sociology,
anthropology, history, etc.) dealing with the history and practice of science. The
term is not especially specific, but it is convenient and there is a tradition of using
it in this way.

constructing, maintaining, and extending the machines (apparatus), technologies, procedures, social organizations, distributed spaces, and collective habits (including oral traditions and embodied craft skills) that make science possible. In the remainder of this chapter, I will outline some of the constraints and social processes that frame scientific account-making, both generally and in psychology.

Cultural and Political Constraints and Processes

These constraints and social processes operate at different levels of social organization, and so scientific account-making must work across a gradient of social sites and actors. At the cultural and political level, for example, Jasanoff (2005) has argued that public policy and other societal factors shape science. These "civic epistemologies" (Jasanoff, 2011, p. 9) vary culturally and nationally and help to constitute regionally specific scientific infrastructures. Jasanoff (2005) outlines, for example, differences in rules for research involving stem cells and genetically modified organisms in Germany, the UK, and the USA. Countless such examples are possible, as scientists have always had to grapple with politics; Galileo did science in the shadow of the church and Oppenheimer in the shadow of the state.

Psychologists operate under, and in response to, the same pressures. Indeed, the most consistent shaping forces in the history of psychological research may well have been the interests of large institutions, particularly governments. Tweney and Budzynski (2000) have argued, for example, that throughout the twentieth century, the "clientele of academic psychology" shifted from "an audience that sought to understand and to better itself" to "industrial, governmental, and social audiences" who "wished to change other selves" (p. 1015). The result was a discipline marked by large-scale assessments and interventions. Morawski (2001a) points to similar dynamics in her discussion of experimental psychology: "techniques and theories in experimental psychology were shaped by their consumers' desires for aggregate data and 'norms' of psychological functioning that were useful in the sorting, classifying, and selecting of individuals" (p. 438).

Nearly any branch of psychological research could furnish instances of such broad political or corporate influence. The shift toward child study in developmental psychology, for example, was heavily influenced by major investments from the Laura Spelman Rockefeller

Memorial (Lomax, 1977). Or, on the darker side of politics, significant funding for research into racial differences in intelligence has been provided by white supremacist groups (Winston, 1998). It is not unusual for political influence to follow the contours of social privilege in this way (i.e., to benefit the interests of dominant groups at the expense of subordinated groups). Marecek, Kimmel, Crawford, and Hare-Mustin (2003), for example, argue that in the postwar era, psychologists contributed to the "domestication" of women professionals,

> [pressing them] into domestic roles by a variety of dubious pronouncements issued under the guise of science. For example, they blamed mothers for a variety of psychological disorders, behavior problems, and social ills in their children (Caplan and Hall-MacCorquodale, 1985). They extolled marriage, motherhood, and subordination to men's interests as criteria of maturity and fulfillment for women. (p. 251)

Gone (2011) points to a more recent regional and political institution-alization of privilege in his discussion of externally imposed "evidence-based" addiction interventions among First Nations groups, an impos-ition mandated by the relevant US government funding body (SAMHSA), but seen as cultural imperialism by members of First Nations groups.

Professional and Disciplinary Constraints and Processes

The constraints and social processes shaping science also operate at the professional and disciplinary levels. The norms, traditions, and fads of professional cultures, for instance, create constraints on acceptable topics, theories, or methods. Knorr-Cetina (1981) notes some of these constraints in her classic lab ethnography: "[research] decisions are based on what is 'hot' and what is 'out,' on what one 'can' or 'cannot' do, on whom they will come up against and with whom they will have to associate by making a specific point" (p. 7). Institutional constraints can also shape what counts as science. Keller (1983), for example, argued that Barbara McClintock's Nobel Prize-winning work was ignored or misunderstood for years because it did not conform to the institutional laboratory structure of genetic research at the time.

Psychology is also shaped by the pressures of disciplinary norms, some of the most pervasive revolving around quantification which, according to Morawski (2011), "affords a set of values in networks of practice, values that include impersonality, restraint, absence of subjectivity, and a particular kind of community of knowers" (p. 263). Peterson (2015) reports the influence of one related norm – namely, the drive for "statistical significance." In one of the child development labs he observed, graduate students were told to "'throw everything' at the babies in order to produce at least one experiment with statistical significance" (p. 6) and lab meetings would routinely focus on any statistically significant findings, lab participants working together to "collectively craft a story" (p. 6) from them.

Even seemingly mundane or peripheral disciplinary norms can have an important influence on the character of a scientific discipline. Traweek (1988), for example, showed that an aggressive rhetorical style was necessary to achieve acceptance in physics. Bazerman (1988) pointed out similar rhetorical influences, showing how the conventions encoded in the *American Psychological Association Style Manual* favored particular approaches to research – that is, generally experimental and quantitative approaches – over others – in particular, qualitative, introspective, or theoretical approaches.

Scientists must also negotiate the social and institutional processes that govern professional organizations and disciplines. They must build alliances and navigate hierarchies, and these hierarchies and alliances will, in turn, shape what kinds of science are possible. Latour and Woolgar (1986), for example, noted how progress in research on the peptide TRF was partially stalled because the reputation and influence of an eminent researcher's early work insulated his conclusions from critique and led other researchers to doubt their own conclusions. Speaking generally, scientists must negotiate (Lynch, 1999) and rhetorically manage (Gilbert and Mulkay, 1984) consensus, and their own authority and credibility within such systems (Livingston, 1999).

Psychologists share this concern with reputation. Peterson (2016), for example, reports psychologists deferring to senior researchers, treating their work as "basically valid" (p. 8) even when it failed to replicate. Also, like other scientists, psychologists will fiercely defend their reputations. Rose (2011) recounts Edward Thorndike's "sense of injustice" and "anger" in "a correspondence with [E. B.] Titchener" (p. 364), because Titchener reviewed Thorndike's book unfavorably. Similarly, Peterson (2015) points to the dust-up between Bargh (1996) and his critics over a failure to replicate a highly cited priming study: "Bargh dismissed the replication and subsequent news coverage as products of 'pay-as-you-go publications and superficial online science journalism' (Bargh 2012). This quickly descended into a squabble between Bargh, the authors of the replication, science bloggers, and online commentators" (p. 1217). Because all scientific knowledge sits within a professional and disciplinary context, such disciplinary politics, norms, structures, rules of governance, and so on necessarily frame and constrain the kinds of questions, methods, and interpretations available to scientists.

Institutional Constraints and Processes

Not just professional politics, but also those of corporations, universities, and legal institutions frame scientific work. Scientists, for example, must deal with institutional constraints related to funding priorities (Fuller, 2000) and gatekeeping practices (Taylor, 1996). A researcher must consider, not just other scientists, but "the provost of the university, the research institute's administrative staff, functionaries of the National Science Foundation, government officials, members or representatives of industry, and the managing editor of a publishing house" (Knorr-Cetina, 1981, p. 82). They must consider not just research design or data analysis, but "available funds, the extent of positive feedback, the general funding policy of a particular state, and the publication and reception of [their] papers" (Latour and Woolgar, 1986, p. 191). Such institutional politics are indigenous to every science, including psychology. Rose (2011), for example, points to J. M. Cattell's firing as a result of university politics; Cattell was "a perpetual critic of [Columbia's] administrative policies" (p. 362), a stance that (along with his opposition to the military draft) led to his dismissal.

In managing all of these constraints, scientists manage hierarchies, bureaucracies, negotiations, budgets, contracts, and so on. Knorr-Cetina (1981) describes an array of practical strategies used to manage the institutional connections to laboratory work. She recounts a lab leader meeting with "the relevant person in Washington" (p. 81) and then modifying a grant proposal; or lab members reading and negotiating contracts with "an industry-sponsored laboratory" (pp. 81) and altering a lab procedure to better serve a particular industry use (as a food additive). She describes a scientist who "applied for a university position" and then "realigned his research (including the use of certain methods), to match the orientation of the appropriate department head" (pp. 81–82). Similarly, "when a representative of industry did not respond enthusiastically to a scientist's results, he began to pursue alternative procedures" (p. 82). Such institutional concerns can thus exert significant influence on domain choice, method, and other "internal" laboratory issues.

This sort of institutional influence can also affect relations with other scientists and the overall development of a particular area of investigation. Knorr-Cetina (1981) quotes a scientist describing the competition for grants: "there are only two strong groups in the area, ourselves and MIT. So, we get every one of their important proposals to review, and they get ours. Of course, they don't want me to go ahead, because money is scarce" (p. 8). There are many such influences on researcher choices, for example selecting "a publisher (and therefore, an audience), as well as various marketing strategies" (p. 13), all of which bring institutional, political, and corporate concerns into everyday lab work.

Psychologists, of course, are no exception. Their research choices are also framed by "the pressures of the academic environment" (Peterson, 2015, p. 4) and external imperatives like the need "not to waste time and resources" (p. 5). Barenbaum and Winter (2003) point to a concrete example of such institutional framing. In their overview of the history of personality assessment in psychology, they note that person-centered assessments – the kind involving detailed narrative case studies – have become common for the assessment of elites, like corporate executives, but not for lower-level workers. They argue that this bifurcated assessment culture is the result of institutional and financial pressures, creating an approach to assessment "stratified, more or less along lines of social power and social class: person-centered for elites ... nomothetic for the masses" (p. 191). Scientists, like everyone else, must work within institutional power structures, so these kinds of economic and political pressures will always shape choices about what and how to conduct research.

Local and Interpersonal Constraints and Processes

Science is shaped not only by such high-level constraints, but also by constraints operating at a more local and interpersonal level – that is, at the level of labs, working groups, partnerships, and so on. Some of these constraints are largely material:

> When we ask, for example, why a particular [scientific] instrument was chosen for a certain purpose, the response may range from "Because it's expensive and rare, and I want to get to know it," to "It's more economical in terms of energy"; from "John suggested it and showed me how to use it," to "It happened to be around, so it was the easiest thing to do"; from "What I had in mind didn't work, so I tried something new," to "They asked me to use this because it's just been bought and we have to show that we needed it." (Knorr-Cetina, 1981, p. 9)

Such constraints can have a significant impact on the shape of scientific work. Latour and Woolgar (1986), for example, noted that TRF was assumed to be a peptide because this was what could be studied with the available chemistry.

Other constraints are more relational, including "peer pressure, [and] the influence of those in authority" (Solomon, 2008, p. 246). Even interpersonal relationships (and histories) can shape lab work. Knorr-Cetina (1981), for example, describes a researcher who proposed sending some lab work to a rival (by the name of "Watkins"). This proposal "garnered little support from his superiors, who had once been members of Watkins' group and still harboured a grudge against him" (p. 44).

Hierarchical relations in labs and research groups also shape how research is done. Latour and Woolgar (1986) describe some of these in the lab they observed: "individuals referred to as doctors read and write in offices in section A while other staff, known as technicians, spend most of their time handling equipment in section B" (p. 45). Power relations, in general, frame lab work, with authority and prestige (Goldman, 1999) filtering how scientific decisions are made: "a concern with names figures prominently in this respect, and debates about the best names with which to associate oneself pervade the laboratory" (Knorr-Cetina, 1981, p. 76).

Peterson (2016) reports similar power dynamics in psychology laboratories, where the lab is "headed by a psychologist who primarily sits in an advisory role" overseeing "postdocs and graduate students [who] are usually the engines of empirical work" (p. 1205). As in other sciences, these hierarchical dynamics shape how science is done. For example, in one lab, a graduate student was "reluctant to run statistics before all the data from all 16 subjects was in" (Peterson, 2015, p. 5). The head of the lab, however, "pulled rank" and told "him that if there was going to be an effect, it should be visible after 12 subjects, so he should run the statistics to find out" (p. 5).

Dewsbury (2003) recounts a fascinating example of such laboratory politics in his description of the Orange Park, Florida animal research laboratory between 1955 and 1957. According to Dewsbury, animosity fulminated between adherents of the traditional conditioning paradigm and their newly invited operant conditioning colleagues, a split that extended beyond the laboratory: "the Fersters socialized primarily with their neighbors, the Nissens, and the other operant psychologists" (p. 257). This division reached its peak in disagreements over the treatment of experimental animals; the traditionalists "deplored the technique of starving down to 80% of body weight as a motivator for chimpanzees" and "there were lots of comments made at weekly staff meetings about the psychology of half-starved animals" (p. 258). At one point,

when the chimps failed to lose weight although on a much-reduced diet, some paranoia set in. At first, it was a joke: maybe Cathy [Nissen] was feeding them spaghetti. But it grew until Charlie and Roger were hanging out at the cages for a good part of the night, spying to make sure that neither Cathy nor Henry went down there to feed the animals. (pp. 258–259)

Though the work of those at Orange Park investigating operant conditioning was productive and well published, the combative atmosphere put an end to the collaboration after only two years.

Such power relationships are endemic to laboratory work and function within a set of interpersonal networks, both within and between labs. Beyond simply encoding power relationships, these networks organize collective labor; for example, lab members help each other "code" data, "'try out' new methods or experiments on each other" (Peterson, 2016, p. 1216), and "help schedule subjects, babysit siblings, and clean up the lab" (p. 1209), among other things. These networks also organize experience and knowledge, including knowledge of unpublished experimental failures, made "known within the lab and across labs through interpersonal networks" (Peterson, 2015, p. 8), "local knowledge regarding the validity or invalidity of articles, methods, and other labs on the basis of previous experience" (p. 7), and insider knowledge about experimental manipulations from colleagues.

These sorts of collaborative (or competitive) practices will, of course, vary between subdisciplines or areas of research. Just as larger political and institutional dynamics frame research questions, practices, and products, the collaborative networks where research is conducted form their own local cultures with their own norms, politics, and institutional practices, all of which also shape what kind of science is possible.

Dispositional and Personal Constraints and Processes

A final type of constraint is the dispositional or personal. These can include particular value or epistemic commitments, dispositions for patience, focus, or other lab "virtues," and, generally, relevant capacities, inclinations, or opportunities that are functions of a unique personal (or collective) history. To even become the focus of science, for example, an idea must be interesting to researchers, and this requires "convincing the research leader of its value, being able to recruit laboratory assistants, finding the necessary equipment, being the first to publish, having time to do the work, etc." (Knorr-Cetina, 1981, p. 59). Latour and Woolgar (1986) also emphasize the importance of interest and individual fulfillment; in the words of one of their informants, "When you have students you cannot ask them to cut brains all the time: you have to give them interesting things to do: you cannot corner them in routine tasks, which will pay off only in five or six years. If they come to your laboratory in order to graduate, they expect to write a few papers, it has to be interesting" (p. 118). Other researchers referenced the need for perseverance, "the brutal force of putting in 60 hours a week" (p. 118), and the need for "recognition from peers" (p. 191) as factors driving scientific productivity.

It is impossible to enumerate the many ways that the values, capacities, and inclinations of scientists frame the kinds of work they do, but the larger point is that these shape not just particular scientists or labs, but science itself. How and what scientists choose to study and the conclusions they draw from their research (as well as the practical applications they pursue or allow) are, at least in part, driven by the idiosyncrasies of individuals and lab communities. According to Latour and Woolgar (1986), for example, TRF became the focus of a particular lab only because they hired a technician with experience in that area. Collins (2010) has argued that such embodied skills and tacit knowledge are a core component of scientific expertise but are not always transferable or teachable; these are, in effect, talents that will travel with those who can develop them. Peterson (2016), for example, discusses a molecular biology student "known for an ability to capture excellent images," a postdoc hired "because he promised to get one of their microscopes to stimulate cells and image at the same time, which other members of the lab had tried and failed to do" (p. 1209), and the importance for developmental psychology researchers to have "skill in handling children" (p. 1210).

In truth, nearly any personal idiosyncrasy could have some impact on how psychology (or science, in general) is done. Edward Thorndike recounts not being able to find accommodation for his animal research until "the 'habitual kindness' of William James who 'harbored my chickens ... in the cellar of his own home'" (Rose, 2011, p. 359) made his research possible. Conversely, "many of Wundt's American students confessed privately that they found him bristly and his ideas stuffy and continued more profitable European studies elsewhere" (Rose, 2011, p. 360) and J. M. Cattell's nasty and arrogant behavior ultimately led to the diminished impact of his journals (Sokal, 2010). Even relatively innocuous inclinations can shape the direction of research, as in Karl Lashley's flirtation with infant research, which ended because he "disliked the babies and found me a rat lab in another building" (Thompson and Zola, 2003, p. 53).

As Polanyi (1958) so cogently argued, science is always conducted from a "personal" position; that is, from the perspective of a particular researcher (or community of researchers), with a unique history and set of capacities, inclinations, and values. These capacities and values constitute a set of personal or dispositional constraints that shape every scientific product in unique ways.

Scientific Account-Making as Everyday Moral Practice

The examples described in this chapter are really just a sampling of the constraints and social and institutional processes framing how research is done, but my task here has been not so much to enumerate all of these as to point to their central role in shaping science. If the art of science is to make accounts that work – that not only report, accredit, and interpret observations, but that can survive gatekeeping practices (and other bureaucracies), build trust, cooperation, and consensus,

mobilize resources, and express (and enact) the commitments underwriting them – then the constraints and processes I have discussed here
are the medium. These are the social and moral geography of science
and every good scientist must learn to navigate them well and responsibly. Indeed, as I have already said, this is the substance of
good science.

This larger point is nicely illustrated by a vignette recounted in
Knorr-Cetina (1981). She describes Roy, an early career scientist
working in a large, prestigious lab:

> Roy had decided to come to the United States after finishing his education
> because it would enable him to get a high-paying, high-prestige position at a
> university or research institute in his own Country. He had chosen a highly
> regarded laboratory because this would enhance his own qualifications, as
> would a letter of recommendation from an esteemed head of a laboratory. He
> used the head of the laboratory to get access to journals, research money and
> "hot" topics of research which he felt would otherwise be denied to him. (p. 85)

These various calculations will not look unusual to anyone involved in
research; they are the everyday practical world of scientific work. They
reflect the ways that science is connected to political, cultural, and
economic systems, to particular institutions and laboratories, to individual needs, commitments, and capacities. They also reflect the social
and bureaucratic processes by which scientists gain resources
and influence.

Roy's story also reflects some of the more mercenary elements of
scientific politics:

> Roy felt that he was being "used" by the head of the laboratory. The
> continuation of his visa and his one-year contracts depended on this man.
> In 1977 and 1978, he was paid less than $10,000 a year, on which he had to
> support a family. He actually wrote the journal reviews which the head of the
> laboratory signed, and he said it was his "ideas" and information that
> resulted in "innovative" research. Needless to say, he conducted all the
> research in a project and supervised the students and technicians in the lab,
> occasionally informing the head of the laboratory of his progress ... While
> he was a co-author of papers published from his research, the decisions
> about what was published when and where were made by the head of the
> laboratory. His name did not appear on the patents to which the research
> gave rise, and presentations of his work were made by the head of the
> laboratory. (pp. 84–85)

In Roy's story, we can see not only some of the various constraints and social processes that shaped his scientific work but from it we can also gain insight into the question that animates this book: namely, *what is good science?* Roy's laboratory made accounts that worked in some respects – they secured funding, publication, prestige – but they clearly did not work in other respects. These accounts were based on the work of, and were largely produced by, individuals lower in a hierarchy (not just Roy, but all those who worked for him) than those who reaped the rewards for them. All of that labor was very poorly compensated, particularly in terms of credit and access to publication and patents, often the true coin of a scientific economy. This was exploitative science – part of a long tradition of cultural privilege – and can hardly be called "good" in these respects.

No doubt, some will argue (as many have) that these personal, political, and moral elements of science work are peripheral and largely unrelated to the true epistemic purposes of science – that is, these may sometimes (as in Roy's case) intrude on scientists, but the quality of the science itself will always depend on more central technical concerns. This chapter is mostly a litany of counter-examples to such claims. Social and historical studies of science show that political, institutional, relational, and dispositional constraints and processes shape scientific questions, methods, and interpretations at least as much as (if not more than) epistemic considerations.

This humanized account of science should not be particularly surprising to any working scientist; to do science is to understand how it grows from and aims toward particular human concerns. "Scientific knowledge is the outcome of community processes and interactions" (Longino, 2002, p. 166, n. 34) and thus every element of science depends upon networks of historically specific, culturally situated humans pursuing particular values and ends. As Morawski (2015) argues with respect to the psychology experiment, "cultural preconditions (e.g., roles, rules of felicity, morals, economic exchanges) are essential to the experiments' execution and success. Cultural know-how grounds experiments from original design to final reports and from recruiting to debriefing subjects" (p. 574). "Put simply, the psychology experiment is a political system complete with economic exchanges and structures of governance (authority)" (p. 588). Of course, this must be true because "the 'ideas' of the laboratory are social occurrences which emerge from interaction and negotiation with others" (Knorr-Cetina, 1981, p. 13) and thus "scientific or cognitive strategies are also political strategies" (p. 22). And this means that good scientists must be not just technicians, but morally, culturally, and politically refined and astute: "the better politicians and strategists they are, the better the science they produce" (Latour and Woolgar, 1986, p. 214).

But science is not just politics or hierarchy, it is also relationship, culture, and community. It is not just better politicians that make better scientists. Better relationships, better moral and ethical traditions, and better communities make better science. Good science is what grows from the continually refined moral practices and continually nurtured moral communities whose complex human architecture is nothing more nor less than science itself.

5 | *Justification*

Good science, then, is a function of good scientific communities, of good relationships, of good faith and of good will. All sciences, we might say, are *human*. This is true in the sense that "science consists in the creative and responsible acts of persons" (Osbeck, 2018, p. ix), but also because science is always *about* people; about their beliefs, desires, histories. This may seem like an odd way to describe science, but if we look carefully at any research report, we will see that it is fundamentally not about molecules, proteins, or memory, but about particular people talking to a particular community.

That report will almost always begin with a story about a community and its shared beliefs; a catalogue of prominent community members and a reporting of their most cherished ideas; a recounting of past ideological conflicts; and a plea for a particular way of framing what matters to that community (i.e., what should be studied next). Most reports (in psychology, at least) will then move to another story about people, this time a description of what a specific group of people did and why (i.e., a "methods" description); a minute recounting of very specific human actions, following highly ritualized narrative conventions. Authors usually then report the "results" of such actions, recounting not a tale about peptides or perceptions, but the story of what particular persons were able to do; what outcomes they could reliably produce and under what circumstances. Finally, at the end of the report, authors share their thoughts; they interpret the story. They say why they think things worked out the way they did, why this is important to them and to their community, their disappointments (i.e., "limitations"), and their hopes for the future (i.e., "future directions").

Nowhere in reports like these are we talking about "nature" or "objects"; we are always reporting our personal and community histories, organized around sets of shared commitments. Certainly, a report can seem to be – and is often carefully constructed to appear as though it is – about priming effects or neurons; but, in fact, all such

57

reports are really about what specific people and communities have *thought* about priming effects, what they've been able to *do* with neurons. Science is a story about what scientists believe, what they have accomplished, what they value; the subject of science is always collective human activity. And this is why "good" science can only be so in virtue of those values, communities, and relationships that constitute that human activity; is only possible when scientists express, attend to, and refine their commitments.

In short, we must all "justify" our work, a word I use here with an eye to its multiple meanings – we justify not simply by providing evidence to support our interpretations, but by justifying, or "trueing," our practices to our shared commitments; by making these just in the full ramifications of that term. When we understand science as human and social – as composed not just of reports or empirical "facts," but of real persons engaged in politically and historically layered persuasion – then it becomes clear that what we must justify is not a claim, but the whole moral architecture of an intrinsically and irreducibly human endeavor. The work of the current chapter is to elaborate this alternative conception of justification and to suggest that, relative to traditional technical conceptions of scientific justification, it is the one more faithful to the real practices, and real moral obligations, of science work in psychology.

A Broader Conception of Scientific Justification

In the context of science, "justification" has generally meant "making a case for" scientific claims, by showing their consistency with empirical facts and accepted scientific theory. But the word has a much richer set of meanings that, I am arguing, we should embrace. The most basic and general meaning of the term "justification" is "to make just" (*iustus* + *facere*), a notion rich with moral (equitable, sincere, proper), religious (upright, righteous, perfect), legal (lawful, impartial, fair), and epistemic (right, exact, true) connotations and usages. Understood in this larger way, I think justification is precisely the right word to describe the basic context of research. Certainly, this is a way of thinking about justification that is more reflective of the human and moral contours of research work.

Speaking very broadly, this whole book could be seen as an argument for treating "justification" of this sort, and not "research methods," as the basic framework for evaluating psychological research. In this book, I am advocating a kind of broadening, and reorienting, of attention; away from a narrow emphasis on technique and toward a more rigorous focus on the fuller range of human contexts that constitute research. Traditional accounts of research practice in psychology have focused on "instrumentation and method," and this "directs attention from the ultimately creative and agentive acts in which evidence is defined, amassed, and used to various ends" (Osbeck, 2018, p. 46). But "evidence must be gathered, interpreted, compared, synthesized, weighed, and applied responsibly, by persons, in line with values" (Osbeck, 2018, p. 109). Scientific labor and scientific interpretations are not fundamentally driven by instrumentation or method, but by interpreting persons in communities of shared commitments.

Good science is thus not merely an extension of correct procedure, nor even of sound theory, but is the product of just actions, relationships, and systems. Science becomes true as we refine those actions, relationships, and systems, making them true to the values, beings, and communities for whom they speak. Science can only be good, and therefore true, when particular scientists act in good faith and in good will, when individuals and communities are held accountable for the abuses and harms of science, when the costs, rewards, and resources of scientific labor are equitably distributed, and so on. When we are training researchers, explaining research, designing research, and reporting research, *justification* – making just, right, and true, our practices – and not "research methods" is what we might call the "core competency."

As I have said often, this way of thinking about justification includes justifying methodological practice, but this too should be understood as a fundamentally moral enterprise. As Brinkmann (2004) has argued, all practices

have certain standards of excellence. They are therefore normative; there are better and worse ways of participating in a practice. Agents who are trying to participate adequately in social practices are at the same time trying to take part in the human goods that are embedded in (or are internal to) those practices. (p. 65)

In this way, methods in science express and instantiate certain values – for example, objectivity, consistency, control, and so on – and part of how we justify science is refining our practices such that they are consistent with those values.

But the "good" of just methods extends well beyond technical competence; methods are not just (nor justifiable) if they are abusive or exploitative. Good design does not just result from clever manipulation; good design comes only when "we accept our accountability for the values and aims that guide our research enterprise and seriously sift and refine the ideals our work promotes" (Richardson, Fowers, and Guignon, 1999, p. 172). As I think will become clear in later chapters, this isn't really a foreign way of framing science; scientists are constantly having to deal with politics, relationships, questions of fairness and justice, and so on; we just don't focus on these questions when we write about, teach, and report scientific work. These questions are treated as peripheral, or perhaps tacit, and I am insisting that they are central and, in fact, the right framework, even for questions of method and fact.

Justifying Research

Assuming we are willing (at least for the sake of argument) to take justification, in the more expansive sense I have outlined, to be the primary work of psychological science, we might justifiably wonder exactly how so wide a mandate could be prosecuted. Here, I argue for two forms of practice that I think travel across all kinds of science and that are simply indispensable to the task of justification – science cannot become good without them. These are what I am calling an open disciplinary politics and a committed research praxis.[1] I draw on a number of thinkers in proposing these terms, but the work of the great twentieth-century ethical philosopher Emmanuel Levinas[2] has most inspired my thinking about these underlying themes.

---

[1] There are likely other values indispensable to good science generally. As Osbeck (2018) notes, philosophers of science have identified a number of values they consider "good for science, whatever the science in question. Examples include integrity and honesty (Lauden, 1984); democratic exchange of views (Longino, 1983); diversity (Harding, 2015); and even passion (Polanyi, 1974/1958)" (p. 35).

[2] Those who know Levinas's work may find this a little strange as his thought is generally framed as primarily about ethics. His major works (particularly *Totality and Infinity* and *Otherwise than Being*), however, centrally address

Levinas does not usually talk specifically about science; instead, he tells a broader story about how knowledge of any kind becomes possible. According to Levinas (1969/1961), "what is proper to knowing ... consists in being able to put itself in question, in penetrating beneath its own condition" (p. 85) – a not unfamiliar characterization of knowledge as critique, skepticism, doubt, and test. Knowing, for Levinas, is not fundamentally about obtaining a correct view of the world, but about putting our comfortable dogmatisms into question and forcing them to survive scrutiny and challenge. But, for Levinas, this "putting ... in question" is not something I can do for myself; it is "produced as the calling into question of the same by the other" (p. 43). In his account, knowledge becomes possible when an unknown[3] Other challenges, resists, "ruptures" my taken-for-granted view of the world. Meaning is an "awakening" that "comes from the Other" (p. 86). Not only knowledge, but my identity as knower, are revealed to me by an Other that resists these. For Levinas, "the essence of reason consists not in securing for man a foundation and powers, but in calling him in question and inviting him to justice" (p. 88).

There are, of course, many ways to respond to this invitation to justice. In fact, Levinas (1997/1981) says, most often we respond by "projecting, or treating this world as one's project" (p. 122). In his language, we "totalize" the Other, reducing her to extensions of my needs, desires, and expectations. This is how we produce ignorance and violence from the encounter with the Other. Genuine knowledge, however, is only possible when I welcome the rupture, become open to it, allow myself to be taught by it. For Levinas, this openness to discovery, to being taught, is not merely passive, but is fundamentally responsive; in his terms, it is "responsibility." The Other awakens me to my ignorance and invites me to redress it, to take up what Levinas calls a "responsibility for the others" which is "is the adventure that bears all the discourse of science and philosophy" (p. 160). To take up this responsibility is to make a commitment to understanding and communication, a "fine risk" that "offers things which are mine to the Other" (p. 76), in the hope of building together a mutual intelligibility. For Levinas, meaningful knowledge requires both this openness

questions of knowing and place these, as I do here, squarely within a moral framework.

[3] And ultimately unknowable in any complete sense.

to uncertainty – to being wrong, to being corrected – and a commitment to the risk and self-exposure of offering what we take to be good, or true, accounts.

Now, I will grant that Levinas's language is somewhat mystical, but these ideas are not so strange nor difficult to understand in the context of science. I think every scientist understands the central role of doubt and openness to critique in the scientific process (in the next section, I will discuss others who have made similar points). Levinas's position is essentially anti-dogmatic, insisting on a world of beings who transcend and resist my knowledge projects, and this critical attitude is also one of the foundations of scientific thinking. Levinas's ideas, I think, enrich and deepen this basic tenet of scientific thinking by showing us how that critical attitude is irreducibly relational; I need others to challenge my comfortable certainties and to pry open the instrumentalities of my privilege. To justify our science, we need not only the communal validation of peer review, replication, and so on, but an open disciplinary politics where various forms of privilege, inequality, and injustice can be interrogated and challenged.

Similarly, a great many have pointed to the value-ladenness of science, to the ways that science is driven by particular commitments and is inseparable from these. Since the advent of science studies, many have come to increasingly acknowledge the committed, value-driven, knower as the most basic and indispensable element of science. Levinas, again, helps us to more fully appreciate the moral and relational labor required of the committed knower. To be good scientists means not just practicing reflexivity and transparency about our positionality, it also means refining our everyday practices such that they become consistent with a set of values that we acknowledge and negotiate within our communities. The everyday work of data collection, report writing, and so on is a kind of moral labor, where we have to hammer out shared commitments amid conflicting needs, beliefs, and priorities. This part of science is mostly invisible in methods textbooks and research reports, and so becomes an effective hiding place for the prejudices, cruelties, and injustices of science and of scientists. To justify our science, then, we need a committed research praxis, one where everyday scientific practices are uncovered in their moral plenitude and refined to become consistent with explicit values.

Together, an open disciplinary politics and a committed research praxis make justification possible because they expose the values upon which scientific labor rests and subject those values to continual scrutiny and refinement. Researchers who approach their work with explicit commitments to particular values, interrogating their own moral stances, as well as those of participants, institutions, funders, and so on can uncover the "tyranny of hidden prejudices" left behind by objectivism. Likewise, a discipline open to critique, one where challenges from the margins can speak as loudly as the status quo, is one where the exceptionalism and institutionalized privilege of scientism can be resisted. Without these kinds of practices, science cannot be justified; we cannot "true" our practices to the values that underwrite them if those values are invisible or unchallengeable; if we have no traditions nor institutional practices for interrogating and refining them.

In the subsequent two chapters, I expand on this basic argument, discussing in detail what I mean, first, by an open disciplinary politics and, second, by a committed research praxis, with the goal of showing their centrality in the justification of psychological research.

6 | *An Open Disciplinary Politics*

In some ways, what I mean by "open" is already the spirit of disciplinary politics in psychology and other sciences. Researchers routinely talk about science as "probabilistic" or inherently "revisable" and generally approach all scientific claims with skepticism, subjecting them to various forms of review, all important elements of an open politics. But there is another side to psychology's (and other sciences') general epistemic culture that reflects a kind of dogmatic scientism; a "closed" attitude toward any critique or reform that comes from outside of accepted disciplinary conventions, norms, and ideologies. Indeed, there are many in psychology who insist on a variety of scientific exceptionalism that privileges certain kinds of questions or methods, and who claim a sort of epistemic certainty that trumps all other, lesser, forms of knowledge (e.g., "armchair reasoning," "subjective" data, and similar pejorative terms). In Chapter 1, I discuss psychology's disciplinary tendencies toward scientism, so I won't repeat that analysis here. Suffice it to say that many psychologists, like other scientists, subscribe to a kind of science fundamentalism and this produces exceptionalist and dogmatic narratives that run counter to the spirit of open critique.

Elsewhere, I (Clegg, 2010) have written about the irony inherent in a dogmatic view of science "as a rhetoric of certainty" (p. 247), given science's cultural status as the paragon of anti-dogmatic, free inquiry. In that analysis, I drew on C. S. Peirce (1935), who criticized the drive for certainty as a kind of conservatism, or "dread of consequences," that is inconsistent with the critical character of science. Instead, he said, science has "always been forwarded by radicals and radicalism ... the radicalism that tries experiments" (p. 61). Peirce saw science as inherently anti-dogmatic, uncertain, and critical: "in order to learn you must desire to learn, and in so desiring not be satisfied with what you already incline to think" (p. 56). I also pointed to the work of Sigmund Koch (1981) who, after years of meticulously documenting the history and state of psychology, decried psychologists' fixation on a "fear-driven species of cognitive constriction, a reduction of uncertainty by denial, by a form of phony certainty achieved by the covert annihilation of the problematic, the complex, and the subtle" (p. 264). He saw the rhetorics of certainty in psychology as social performances interfering with the truly scientific work of critique. This was his prescription for the dogmatism that ails us: "if significant knowledge is the desideratum, problems must be approached with humility, methods must be contextual and flexible, and anticipations of synoptic breakthrough must be held in check" (p. 268).

Dogmatism, in other words, is the enemy of good science, and uncertainty, humility, skepticism, and an openness to continued questioning are the proper states of healthy scientific inquiry. Uncertainty, we might say, is not a problem to be solved, but a positive condition, a necessary *pre*condition to good science. If science depends on a constant critique to refine its claims and practices, then humility, flexibility, and (the term I am using here) openness are indispensable in the production of meaningful knowledge.

Of course, as Levinas (among others) emphasizes, that healthy state of open critique is not something that I can produce in solitude. Openness and critique require others, come from others who have the standing to challenge my comfortable dogmatisms. This is not a new idea among philosophers of science. At least since Popper, there has been a general recognition that "improvement" or "correction" in science is only possible in collective, rather than individual (or even purely rational), processes. Communal practices refine science across time, place, and person. As Longino (2002) puts it, "the satisfaction of goals of inquiry is not ascertained privately, but by evaluation with respect to shared values and standards" (pp. 130–131).

As I alluded to earlier, in many important respects, traditions of practice in psychological research also inscribe this commitment to collective critique. Nearly all psychological research, for example, makes it into the professional literature only after it is scrutinized by professional peers on review and editorial boards, and influential claims are regularly debated and tested in further research. More recently, many researchers and commentators have also begun to draw attention to some of the gaps in this process of professional critique (see Morawski, 2019; Wiggins and Christopherson, 2019), including specific cases of plagiarism or data falsification, and general problems with insufficient replication, improper use of statistical logics, and so on. The fact that these issues register as problems and that at least some are attempting to address them shows a general disciplinary commitment to an open politics. I think that most psychologists agree, at least in principle, that the practices and claims of psychological researchers should be open to critique in consistent and structurally embedded ways.

An important question to consider, however, is what forms of open and structurally embedded critique are necessary for good science. I suspect that it wouldn't be hard to find some agreement on the necessity of institutionalized ethics and editorial review. There might be a bit more discord around some of the proposals flowing from the Open Science movement, or from those critical of statistical usage in science. Even in these cases, however, I suspect that psychologists could find some new consensus around how to monitor and encourage replication, how to address under- or over-reporting, or how to reform suspect statistical practices. These are all important elements of an open disciplinary politics that could probably find broad endorsement.

However, as Sandra Harding, Helen Longino, and others (see Chapter 2) have argued, attempts to institutionalize checks on scientific practice will be fundamentally inadequate if these do not take into account the broader cultural and social power dynamics within which science sits. An open disciplinary politics requires not just collective attention to epistemic norms but to the often "tacit patterns of thought" (Longino, 2002, p. 204) and action that govern how these are formulated and legislated. The "rules" of science, whether explicit or implicit, are arbitrated in social interactions governed by individual and community values: "Establishing what the data are, what the descriptive categories and their boundaries are, what counts as acceptable reasoning, which assumptions are legitimate and which not becomes a matter of social interactions as much as a matter of interaction with the material world" (pp. 204–205). These social interactions, at least partially, determine the character of science but they are usually hidden and, as history has shown (see Chapter 3), will often favor those in positions of influence and exploit those with fewer social protections. An adequately open disciplinary politics is one where such structural inequalities can be interrogated and challenged.

Longino (2002) has argued for a particular set of disciplinary norms that would allow for such "critical interaction" (p. 204). This is her summary of those norms:

Those assumptions are epistemically acceptable which have survived critical scrutiny in a discursive context characterized by at least four conditions. These conditions are (1) the availability of venues for and (2) responsiveness to criticism, (3) public standards (themselves subject to critical interrogation), and (4) tempered equality of intellectual authority. (p. 206)

Longino's argument is that

A diversity of perspectives is necessary for vigorous and epistemically effective critical discourse. The social position or economic power of an individual or group in a community ought not determine who or what perspectives are taken seriously in that community. Where consensus exists, it must be the result not just of the exercise of political or economic power, or of the exclusion of dissenting perspectives, but a result of critical dialogue in which all relevant perspectives are represented. (p. 131)

This access to authority and the right to be heard, regardless of status, is what Longino calls the equality of intellectual authority (which should, according to Longino, be tempered based on some criteria relating to scientific qualifications). Without this equality, she argues, social privilege overdetermines scientific practices and discourses, a problem both epistemological and moral: "the exclusion of women and members of certain racial minorities from scientific education and the scientific professions constitutes not only a social injustice but a cognitive failing" (p. 132).

Of course, acknowledging the importance of such equality is wholly insufficient without structural means to realize it, and this is why, according to Longino (2002), we must "take active steps to ensure that alternative points of view are developed enough to be sources of criticism and new perspectives. Not only must potentially dissenting voices not be discounted; they must be cultivated" (p. 132). Some of the steps she advocates include balancing the visibility and prestige of mainstream and critical viewpoints in prominent journals and other professional venues; and fashioning public, explicit standards, or values, against which competing accounts can be evaluated.

How, or whether, such recommendations could be realized in psychological science is an open question, but the larger point is that they aim at an equality indispensable, in both moral and epistemological terms, to good science. A science whose politics are open to critique across the whole range of qualified contributors (and, particularly, to critiques of structurally embedded inequality and injustice) is a science where dogma, inertia, and power do not dominate but are instructed and corrected by the broadest possible range of relevant perspectives. Obviously, the disciplinary structures that house psychological research nourish various forms of inequality and so have some distance to cover before such a truly open politics becomes possible. That said, generations of researchers and theorists, primarily working from historically marginalized social positions, have developed practices meant to foment such equality and to redress the worst power imbalances in research practice. There is much from these traditions that could, if taken seriously, contribute to a genuinely open disciplinary politics in psychology. I have space for no more than a sampling of such work, so I will mention only two of the richest examples (and these only briefly): decolonizing and feminist frameworks.

Decolonizing Frameworks

Decolonizing frameworks, flowing primarily from scholars in/from the Global South, are rooted in a history of resistance to colonization as well as to the larger coloniality embedded in various institutions and practices, including science. Decolonizing analyses consider "how disciplines, territories, nations, and empires acquire a colonizing stance – a stance that creates a power structure in which other views, perspectives, and ways of thinking become undermined, made invisible, and eviscerated" (Bhatia, 2019, p. 111). As already discussed in Chapter 3, scientists and psychologists have been complicit in this colonial project and, in various ways, have embedded the biases of that coloniality. Decolonizing scholars seek to uncover these biases and they also suggest strategies for addressing the inequality and error that flow from them.

A key starting point for many decolonizing approaches is a critical analysis of science, "an effort to 'provincialize' (Chakrabarty, 2000) its historical origins, identify its power structures, and resituate it as a local discipline" (Bhatia, 2019, p. 112). When research practices can be seen as rooted in specific histories, politics, value orientations, commitments, and so on, then we can evaluate the relevance of these commitments, and the practices that flow from them, for other times, places, and peoples. This sort of situated critique also opens up possibilities for shaping psychological research practices to the needs and commitments of diverse communities, "a psychology in which questions of social justice, centering the voices of the marginalized, and access to public goods could become central to its mission, a mission which speaks to the lives of the majority of the world's population" (Bhatia, 2019, p. 110).

In general, decolonizing approaches seek to center those experiences and communities that have been historically marginalized by mainstream Western science. This is partly a matter of justice – that is, of representing those that have been disenfranchised – as well as an attempt at better reflecting the world's population, very little of which is represented by those who have conducted, and participated in, psychological research (Henrich, Heine, and Norenzayan, 2010). But focusing on marginalized experiences is also an epistemological strategy meant to counter the dogmatism of ingrained privilege. Ignacio Martín-Baró, a liberation theorist working primarily in El Salvador, emphasized this point: "Martín-Baró urged psychologists to recognize the epistemological value of marginalized perspectives as a tool for de-ideologizing conventional knowledge and providing a firmer conceptual basis for liberatory action" (Adams, Dobles, Gómez, Kurtiş, and Molina, 2015, p. 218). For Martín-Baró, and other liberation and decolonizing theorists, privileging "the epistemological position of people in oppressed or marginalized conditions" not only helps to counter dogma and institutional inertia, but also to facilitate "a participatory research ethos that emphasizes praxis over sterilized theory" (p. 216) and "forms of knowledge that resonate with local realities and better serve local communities" (p. 223).

Though this is the thinnest of introductions to decolonizing approaches, I hope it is still clear how such approaches provide great insight into the practical project of developing a more open disciplinary politics. It is not by chance that those on the excluded and oppressed margins have seen most clearly the moral and epistemological consequences of an insular and values-opaque science; nor is it coincidence that they are at the vanguard of developing practices to counteract those consequences. Psychology could move much closer to an open politics, to a disciplinary structure that works to counteract epistemic and moral imbalances, if we "provincialized" and critically situated the psychology curriculum and interrogated and exposed the local and practical values underpinning it; if, in publishing, governance, hiring, and the disbursement of funds, we privileged marginalized and oppressed perspectives and so allowed these to deconstruct and correct our ingrained biases.

Feminist Approaches

Similar to decolonizing theorists, feminist thinkers have long pointed to the ways that power imbalances in science are not only injustices but productive of misunderstanding and error (see Chapter 3 for discussion of some examples). Feminist theorists have also proposed ways of addressing such imbalances, most often focusing on "addressing the limitations of one's position, seeking different standpoints, and employing complex collaborative methods that better enable representation of multiple perspectives" (Morawski, 2001b, p. 65). Helen Longino, Sandra Harding, Donna Haraway, and many others have argued that the intentional and structural integration of multiple perspectives is indispensable to meaningful knowledge (and, some have argued, to objectivity). Different perspectives, or standpoints, correct the insularity of not just androcentric science but of any kind of sedimented privilege.

Feminist theorists have advocated a number of different strategies for integrating such attention to perspective. One of the most important of these is to foreground critique as integral to inquiry. As Morawski (2001b) has argued, "no study, however honorable its politics, should be exempted from critical analysis" (p. 69). Such analysis includes, among other things, "locating psychological phenomena in their historical, cultural and geographical contexts, with an attention to how these contexts structure and nuance these phenomena differently" (Burman, 2012, p. 653), as well as evaluating the political contexts, ends, and effects of particular knowledge practices and disciplinary structures. As Longino (2002) points out, a commitment to critique of this sort would require allocating to critical analyses a great deal more space and prestige in prominent research journals.

Erica Burman (2012) also points out that such critical analysis requires collaboration across disciplinary regionalities as this helps "to highlight how what is typically claimed to be a stable, general, even timeless and universal phenomenon has arisen at a very particular time and place" (p. 653). Collaboration and interdisciplinarity, in general, are often advocated as strategies to layer into our work multiple (and corrective) perspectives. The perspectives of non-scientists, including "participants and other interested parties" (p. 653), are also valued as sources of perspective and wisdom, a commitment that requires power-sharing across the social gradients of research practice.

Considering the recommendations of feminist and decolonzing thinkers, it is clear that they share much, including overlapping histories and theorists. Their strategies for addressing power, privilege, and insularity in the research process are complimentary, something that can be seen, for example, in the work of the Public Science Project (PSP):

At the PSP, we build research teams that are deeply heterogeneous by standpoint, perspective, status and line of vision and tilt our research questions, as Ignacio Martin-Baro (1996) argued, "with a preference for the poor." By so doing, we migrate Sandra Harding's (1993) notion of strong objectivity into our projects, valuing the deep deliberation among varied perspectives to sculpt research questions, designs, methods, analytic strategies, and determine products by delicately exploring rather than denying the subjective interests of researchers/community members/activists. (Fine, 2016, p. 358)

As part of this work, Michelle Fine (2016) suggests other commitments that also challenge privileged knowledge positions, including the mandate that "research on oppression must be linked to research on accumulation of privilege" and the insistence that "research is most valid and 'of use' when designed by/alongside and in the interest of social justice movements and then circulated through lawsuits, academic papers, community performances, social media, and products of meaningful engagement with community life and movement actions" (p. 358).

These various commitments and practices, born from generations of resistance, embody precisely what I mean by the collective work of justification. By insisting on structural, historical, and cultural critique, by reaching across disciplinary (and other) boundaries, and by working to distribute power and resources across gradients of privilege, feminist and decolonizing theorists, activists, and researchers have helped to pry open the hard edges of disciplinary and cultural tradition and make psychology more genuinely "correctable." Practices like these, that reach beyond the merely technical and into the complex social structures that constitute science, are what make possible a truly anti-dogmatic, or open, psychological science.

Epistemic Citizenship

It perhaps goes without saying that, while the dominant discourses and practices in psychological research reflect some aspects of an open politics (e.g., peer review), this is less true for those practices that challenge existing power structures (e.g., privileging marginal perspectives). This is unsurprising given existing power dynamics, in the discipline and in larger society, that continue to support a status quo reproducing race, national, and gender (among other) marginalities (see Chapter 3). If we can grant the value of an open disciplinary politics, however, then this sort of exclusionary status quo presents problems for anyone trying to do good science. Even if you or I value critical discourse and diversity of perspective as indispensable to a responsive, relevant, just, and non-dogmatic science, this will have little effect if the disciplinary structures that work against these remain unchallenged. "The status quo is a social conspiracy against the powerless, and nothing is more feeble against a social conspiracy than individual defiance" (Weisstein, 1993, p. 242).

The kind of discipline where genuine justification is possible – where an open disciplinary politics challenges and corrects power and inertia – can only become (and remain) possible with collective political, and not just laboratory or interpretive, labor. You and I can do good science only insofar as our disciplinary structures permit it, and thus good science is a matter not only of individual data collection and analysis, but of *epistemic citizenship* – that is, of collective political work that challenges and transforms the disciplinary structures framing psychological knowledge. Such transformation, as Naomi Weisstein says, requires power, and so takes place "on review panels and in journal article reviews ... on dissertation committees," and wherever resources are controlled and distributed; places where we can use "gatekeeping ... [as] a powerful tool to shape the larger landscape of the profession" (Stewart and Shields, 2001, p. 305).

Epistemic citizenship, then, requires disciplinary participation, savvy, and influence, not generally things taught in a methods class, nor acknowledged in a research report. The invisibility of such activity, however, does nothing to diminish its importance in determining the character of science. The objectivist narrative obscures such moral and human labor, but this only abets the consolidation of power within an unchallenged status quo. An open disciplinary politics – one where our hidden histories, commitments, and ingrained forms of privilege are explicitly challenged, where humility and uncertainty are cherished scientific values, and where we each take seriously an epistemic citizenship dedicated to such values – is one where psychological researchers embrace that moral labor as indispensable to the justification of good science.

7 | A Committed Research Praxis

If we take an open disciplinary politics as essential to the justification of psychological research, then we might reasonably wonder what kinds of knowledge are possible under such an insistent critique. Certainly, universal, synoptic, and monolithic visions of psychological inquiry – the textbook accounts of unchallenged "facts" about "human nature" – become untenable. A radically open critique inevitably exposes the regionalities of knowledge; the ways that they reflect particular communities, particular interests, particular moments in history or geography. So, what kind of knowledge remains when the absolutes of a purely naturalistic narrative are provincialized?

This question, or at least some version of it, is an ancient one: what can we believe when all assumptions are questioned? Meno, representing the sophists, accused Socrates of this sort of critique: "Socrates, before I even met you, I used to hear that you are always in a state of perplexity and that you bring others to the same state" (Plato, trans. 1981, p. 68). And Socrates did not deny it: "I myself do not have the answer when I perplex others, but I am more perplexed than anyone when I cause perplexity in others" (p. 69). Socrates embraced the uncertainty, the perplexity, brought about by his questions. Unlike the sophists, however, he did not take relativism to be the inevitable or natural result of such uncertainty. He was still committed to the search for true accounts: "I do not insist that my argument is right in all other respects, but I would contend at all costs both in word and deed as far as I could that we will be better men, braver and less idle, if we believe that one must search for the things one does not know" (p. 76).

Socrates acknowledged the perilous state of critical inquiry, while still insisting on a commitment to the truest and best accounts, and this sort of *commitment amidst uncertainty* is precisely the state of good scientific inquiry. In *Personal Knowledge*, his landmark account of scientific practice, Michael Polanyi (1958) argues that scientists must "accept commitment as the only relation in which we can believe something to be true" (p. 328). He rejects the notion of science as the pursuit of an unassailable, person-independent, and absolute truth beyond critique. Scientists, Polanyi claims, do not deal in certainties and must "abandon all efforts to find strict criteria of truth and strict procedures for arriving at the truth" (p. 328). Instead, scientists commit, in "an act of hope, striving to fulfill an obligation" (p. 67), to the best and truest accounts they can give.

As I suggested in the previous chapter, certainty is not the goal of science; certainty is merely a failure of imagination. Commitment, on the other hand, is where the best scientific labor aims. The scientist looks for the best accounts, the best models, the best predictions, the best practices to take a chance on, but it is always a *chance*, "a fine risk" as Levinas calls it, an uncertain but not arbitrary commitment. A scientist, Polanyi (1958) says, "decide[s] what to believe, yet there is no arbitrariness in his decision. For he arrived at his conclusions by the utmost exercise of responsibility. He has reached responsible beliefs, born of necessity, and not changeable at will" (p. 328). A scientist works within, and is responsible to, a set of both tacit and explicit commitments, and the fact that these are context-dependent and never certain (rather than universal and unassailable) does not make them soft, unreasoned, or arbitrary; they are the best possible product of the best possible science.

Thus, to privilege commitment over certainty is not to advocate arbitrariness, nor an absence of standards by which to evaluate scientific practice; it is to insist on the contextual nature of scientific standards: "the contextualist interpretation holds that justification is neither arbitrary nor subjective, but is dependent on rules and procedures immanent in the context of inquiry" (Longino, 2002, p. 92). Scientific standards, in other words, inhere within the historically and culturally contingent contexts of scientific work. Historically, some (e.g., Latour, 2004) have feared a contextualist account of scientific justification, but such fears have often "neglect[ed] ... the important distinction between the possibility of universally and eternally binding scientific methods ... and standards of any kind" (Osbeck, 2018, p. 24). Certainly, we must be able to distinguish between valid and suspect scientific claims, but this does not mean that there is some universal, "view from nowhere," set of criteria that we can apply to all scientific practice. Instead, scientists must exercise judgment within a set of community-level standards, or value commitments, that determine the acceptability of scientific claims: "standards may be locally established (relevant to the aims of the science and research project) but remain binding. They are enforced within the system (e.g., the particular science sanctioned within a particular historical period) in which the knowledge-oriented practice is situated" (p. 24). Those commitments can be quite variable across different scientific communities but this is because those different communities have different goals, processes, values, and so on. These commitments *should* be variable because the contexts that define them are variable.

The chief implication of this line of argument is that fidelity to a set of context-dependent (individual, relational, communal, disciplinary, societal) commitments is ultimately what determines the value of scientific practices and claims. Science is "a form of committed social practice" (Richardson et al., 1999 p. 305), and so is justified in terms of those commitments underwriting it. It therefore follows that the justification of science requires discourses and practices designed to articulate, evaluate, and refine shared values, as well as to assess how well those values are realized in particular instances of scientific labor or production. From the local level of the lab to the more general levels of discipline or society, we must know how to articulate, refine, and arbitrate our values. As Osbeck (2018) argues, "recognition that values are inescapable in psychological science is necessary but not sufficient. There is also a need for ongoing and open discussion and negotiation of values" (p. 34).

This argument is perhaps not so radical if we consider only those values most commonly advocated in accounts of science – for example, empirical adequacy, parsimony, and so on. However, as I have argued throughout this book, not only are so-called "social" values (like good faith or justice) determinative of good scientific processes, but even so-called "epistemic" values (like empirical adequacy) are always at least partially social in their character, and their arbitration within scientific communities is entirely social (i.e., carried out in critical discourse among human participants). The context within which scientific work must be evaluated is thus not merely epistemic, but includes the more expansive range of values implied in the notion of "justification" (see Chapter 5). The work of the current chapter is to outline this broad conception of values arbitration, or what I am calling a committed research praxis.

By "praxis" I mean not only a formalized set of rules or procedures (the "methods" of most textbooks and research courses), but also the much larger and more complex set of discourses and practices, both tacit and explicit, through which we compose, conduct, and arbitrate research and its products. A research praxis is not just composed of techniques for data collection and analysis; it is also composed from the institutional habitus of grant and ethics review, the relational shadings of collaboration and power in the lab, the lexical residues of methods instruction, the rhetorical conventions of reporting, and of countless other moments of human engagement and interpretation. When I am arguing that a "committed" research praxis is essential to scientific justification, I am arguing (along with Longino, Osbeck, Richardson, Harding, Slife, and many others) for an explicit engagement in articulating, across all of these technical, social, and political sites, our shared commitments and evaluating the degree to which our practices reflect those commitments. In the remainder of this chapter, I will argue that one primary way that this is done in science is by: (1) asking questions (2) together (3) in a place.

Asking Questions

What I mean by "asking questions" is something very literal: I am referring to a particular person voicing a genuine question, to another, particular, person about something of importance to a shared community. This kind of questioning creates critical engagement; it induces and requires dialogue; and it is anchored in real community (points I will return to below). It is also an invitation to ongoing consideration and negotiation, rather than a static normative statement. Good science requires continual moral attention, and the perpetual, culturally and structurally ingrained, asking of genuine moral questions is a powerful way to continually articulate, evaluate, and refine our scientific commitments.

As researchers, we can ask questions, first, of ourselves and of our research. This can be done in all sorts of ways, but there already exist some vocabularies and forms of practice, originating mostly in qualitative and community-oriented forms of research, for engaging in such values explication, usually coming under names like reflexivity and transparency.

Historically, reflexivity has been "narrowly viewed as the analytic attention to the researcher's role" (Dowling, 2006, p. 8), involving "continuous self-critique and self-appraisal" to "explain how his or her own experience has or has not influenced the stages of the research process" (p. 8). Understood in this way, "reflexivity is not usually seen as connected with ethics" (Guillemin and Gillam, 2004, pp. 274–275), but, instead, as "a way of ensuring rigor" (pp. 274–275). A number of theorists, however, have extended the concept of reflexivity to apply to the moral and ethical examination of research activities. Guillemin and Gillam (2004), for example, have suggested a kind of ethical reflexivity, where a researcher continually assesses whether his or her "practice is actually embodying his or her principles" (p. 276). This reflexivity includes attention to "the ethical dimensions of ordinary, everyday research practice," "sensitivity to what we call the 'ethically important moments' in research practice, in all their particularities," and "having or being able to develop a means of addressing and responding to ethical concerns if and when they arise in the research" (p. 276).

Duffy and Chenail (2009) have suggested a similar kind of ethical attention to the research values of "fidelity; openness and transparency; care for the research participants; competence; beneficence; and statistical, practical, and clinical significance" (p. 33). As I am doing here, they also suggest that researchers ask themselves questions as a way of evaluating their research; these includes questions like "Has the researchers' context been shared so that questions of conflicts of interest and commitment can be addressed?" (p. 34); or "Is there evidence that research participants have been respected?" (p. 35).

Tuval-Mashiach (2017) has also applied this sort of values interrogation to the notion of transparency, another concept typically associated with rigor and replicability. Tuval-Mashiach argues that transparency is not merely about documenting procedure, but also about revealing how researchers address their various responsibilities. These, it is argued, are embedded in relationships with participants, readers, and colleagues, all of which "are part of that which the researcher needs to bear in mind and take responsibility for during the research process and afterward" (p. 128).

Most who advocate this sort of values reflexivity or transparency have suggested that it be realized (or at least reported) through some kind of "auditing" process, involving the "documentation of all the decisions, ideas, and dilemmas the researcher had, including feelings and considerations he or she made along the way, as well as notes on interactions with participants and colleagues" (Tuval-Mashiach, 2017, p. 131). In the 2018 APA guidelines for qualitative reporting, for example, Levitt, Bamberg, Creswell, Frost, Josselson, and Suárez-Orozco (2018) suggest that researchers should be

... making explicit how investigators' values guided or limited the formation of analytic questions ... In addition to describing the phenomena, data sources, and investigators in terms of their location, era, and time periods, qualitative researchers seek to situate these factors in relation to relevant social dynamics. A description of their position within a social order or key relationships can aid readers in understanding and transferring a study's findings. (pp. 29–30)

Keeping track of and reporting "this transparency provides the reader with information that permits an understanding of their goals" (p. 29).

While the proponents of reflexivity and transparency describe traditions of practice conducive to moral attention in science, there are certainly many other ways to engage in such attention; and such attention is just as important in quantitative as in qualitative traditions. The larger point here is that in a committed research praxis, we need ways to ask of ourselves and our research serious moral questions. This sort of sustained moral attention is the substance of a committed research praxis and is essential to the process of justifying science.

Together

One obvious limitation to traditional accounts of reflexivity is that these focus on self-analysis while the moral context of research (and, indeed, of essentially all human activity) is always a relational and communal one. Longino (2002), who also advocates reflexivity in her social account of knowledge, notes this limitation: "the social account builds reflexivity in, but does not leave it up to individual self-examination (which is often blind to the deepest assumptions). Awareness of values and presuppositions is imposed on inquirers through interactions with those who do not share them" (p. 165). Reflexivity, like openness, is really only possible in community. Critical and standpoint theorists have repeatedly pointed to the ways that privilege and positionality blind us to the perspectives of others. We only really become reflexive about our values, our privilege, and so on when we are forced to see them through the eyes of those who don't already participate in them. What's more, "values" are never purely individual, so reflecting on and refining these is only meaningful in the context of the communities where they reside.

Perhaps another way to think about this point is to acknowledge that the asking of genuine questions requires interlocutors, and so a truly committed research praxis requires communal values engagement, and not simply an individual reflection on values or bias. Elsewhere, Brent Slife and I (Clegg and Slife, 2005) have argued that the task of evaluating scientific research could be most meaningfully understood not as the consolidation of abstract propositional frameworks, but as the negotiation of concrete, motivated, culturally and historically situated interpretive practices – that is, as an expression of a communitary ethos. What we claimed, and what I am arguing here, is that the value (including the truth value) of scientific claims is determined by their relation to these local communal contexts of responsibility.

It is thus community values and practices, and not merely personal ones, that we reflect on and refine in a committed research praxis. To be a committed knower is, at least in part, a matter of becoming responsive – or, to use Levinas's term, "responsible" – to others and to the needs and values of one's communities. Such community responsibility can be developed in many ways and will, of course, vary significantly depending on how we define our communities. For example, some participatory researchers (e.g., Halling, Kunz, and Rowe, 1994) have advocated a collective epistemic responsibility through explicitly dialogical theory development and data analysis – that is, the development of research models and questions, as well as the analysis of data, in discursive collaboratives. Finlay (2002) has called this a kind of "collaborative reflexivity," where researchers reflect on the processes of research together and take "the opportunity to hear, and take into account, multiple voices and conflicting positions" (p. 220).

Some research traditions, notably Participatory Action Research (PAR), have defined research communities more expansively, including those outside of academia, and have democratized elements of research practice typically reserved for credentialed researchers. In PAR projects, researchers and community members help to

... determine what questions to ask and which methods to use. Together they develop or adapt the research instruments, carry out the research, and take part in analyzing the results ... [T]he community members themselves own the results of the research and can determine how the information is to be used in addressing the concerns they have articulated. (Brydon-Miller, 2001, p. 81)

Cultivating such communal responsibility requires a whole range of social and political skills and commitments, including "a willingness to be scrutinized and held to declared standards of practice" (Chataway, 2001, p. 242), patience over "a lengthy consensus-building process with people in the context" (p. 241), and general skills in mediation, communication, dialogue, and so on. This whole process is explicitly value-laden, and "convictions ... become central and mutually acknowledged components of the research process, and the research process itself can be seen and evaluated in terms of its ability to generate broad community participation and on its political, social, and economic impact" (Brydon-Miller, 2001, p. 80).

There are many other forms of practice that make explicit a commitment to collective responsibility in research, but this brief sketch suffices to outline the kinds of collective question-asking conducive to a committed research praxis. Whatever our approach to research, we cannot adequately justify our science if we do not interrogate our shared values and evaluate the degree to which our work reflects these; and, as these values are the product of a community and of its collective commitments, our responsibilities to them can only be arbitrated within those communities. Asking (and attempting to answer) moral questions together, and not merely of ourselves, opens the possibility for that collective responsibility.

In a Place

Of course, who we talk to, and who we answer to, in the development and evaluation of our research activities profoundly shapes the kind of moral questions we ask and are required to answer. Most often, the communities and interests that researchers respond to are those with oversight and resources. This is why the kinds of ethical questions most often asked of researchers concern institutional risk (confidentiality of records, consent, etc.), financial risk (appropriate use of funds, statements of impact, etc.), or guild-related questions about scientific rigor (validity, reliability, etc.). The many locally relevant moral questions that arise in the conduct of research – for example, the treatment of support and research staff, the financial, emotional, and environmental impacts of research on the communities and physical spaces where it is conducted, the fair representation of participant perspectives, and so on – are much less likely to be subject to review, reporting, or other scrutiny. Thus, the communities we respond to in our work as researchers are not always the ones upon whom our research bears, nor are they always the communities who bear its costs, impacts, or risks.

This sort of *dis*location – the extraction of research from its local moral contexts and its plotting within the concerns and commitments of distant and powerful interests (large institutions, funding agencies, scientific disciplines, etc.) – is not accidental. It is an essential element of an objectivist approach to science. Most researchers in psychology (and other sciences) are seeking to produce general, or generalizable, knowledge – knowledge that will "scale" beyond a particular local instance of research and apply to humans generally, or at least more broadly than one particular community. This approach to research is naturalized in discussions of psychological science. It is, in fact, simply construed *as* science (see Clegg, 2016). But, of course, it is not a coincidence that a generalizable science serves the ends of the large institutional forces that fund science. Most research in psychology (and elsewhere) is funded by governments, corporations, and other large institutions that require "scalable" techniques or products (see Chapter 3).

Obviously, the interests of those that fund psychological research are important elements of the general ethos shaping the values of psychological research, but they are not the only interests, nor should those interests be hidden behind a veil of neutralist objectivism (see Chapter 2). A genuinely committed research praxis requires moral attention to the full historical and material context that produces and shapes specific research activities. All research happens in a particular temporal, geographic, and political place; a place that shapes what is possible and what matters. Dislocation from that local particularity into decontextualized generalities obscures the moral context of research and makes difficult (or even impossible) the disclosure and refinement of those commitments driving science work.

Asking moral questions together, then, is inadequate if that conversation is abstracted from the localities of a particular place. Genuine moral attention requires attention not just to questions, but to who is asking those questions and for what purposes, whose questions are not being heard and why, the political and institutional history of those questions, and so on. Some have argued that such "an analysis of the context and political environment surrounding the researcher's study is a part of reflexivity" (Dowling, 2006, p. 15) or, at least, should be. Erica Burman (2006) argues that this approach to "reflexivity involves returning from the micropolitics of the research encounter to instead analysing the political economy of its production" (p. 327). Whether or not we call it "reflexivity," this sort of localist, material, political, and historical analysis of how, why, and by whom research is produced is a necessary component of a committed praxis.

Moral attention to the local context of research, however, is not just a matter of interrogating or disclosing that context; it is also a matter of attending to the moral dilemmas and duties that inhere in the places where we do research. These are countless (Part III of this book will be mostly devoted to describing some of these in psychological research) and include political, cultural, environmental, and interpersonal (among other) relationships and commitments not usually discussed in research instruction or reports. Linda Tuhiwai Smith (2013) has pointed to some of these in her discussion of the research encounter. She does so by asking questions of those interested in research with indigenous groups, but her questions reveal the moral shape of all kinds of research places (each of her questions is illuminating, but for brevity, this is only a sampling):

What intellectual, emotional, ethical, political and spiritual preparation have you had? ... Where have you come from? What are your geo-political origins and touchstones? ... Who is your community? ... Who are your research ancestors? ... Did they come here before? If so, what mark did they make? ... Whose voices best represent your community? ... How can they be known by this new community? (can they call and speak?) ... How do you "see" the people you are moving towards? ... What hope and possibility do you bring on to this space? ... Can you see them in their history and place? ... Can you see their hope and possibility? ... What does this meeting mean for you? ... Is it the means to the end? (p. 17)

These kinds of questions, of course, reflect and respond to the colonial history of research on indigenous communities, research where local communities were exploited and misrepresented, and where the concerns and perspectives of local people, as well as the sacredness and sustainability of local places, were ignored. But these questions point more broadly to the moral valences and affordances of all places where research might be conducted. Research places are always an intersection of commitments and responsibilities both very personal (e.g., commitments to good faith and good will) as well as much larger and older than the particular people who represent them (commitments to coloniality, sustainability, etc.), and a committed praxis requires that we attend to these together.

Attending to such morally complex questions can be difficult, particularly as moral responsibility is inherently local, relational, and particular, while research discourses and practices in psychology (and other sciences) are often understood and prosecuted on a more general and industrial scale. Indeed, research production in psychology is increasingly structured and audited under neoliberal logics favoring efficiency, scale, and "the relation of scientific research to production and commerce whose consequence is [the] privatization of information and ideas" (Longino, 2002, p. 129). Such logics make moral attention difficult because they displace local decision-making about the purposes and impacts of research (see Ostenson, Clegg, and Wiggins, 2017; Clegg, Wiggins, and Ostenson, 2020; Morawski, 2019; Sugarman and Thrift, 2017) and replace these with a kind of audit culture (Shore, 2008), a "scientism that … mobilises the pseudo-democratic discourses of transparency and accountability" (Burman, 2012, p. 656) in the service of purely institutional values (scale, efficiency, etc.).

Asking moral questions together in a localized, context-sensitive way thus also requires some resistance to the neoliberalizing forces that extract research from its local moral context. This sort of resistance could take many forms, including de-commoditizing and de-corporatizing research through a disinvestment from (particularly large) grant culture, de-growth in the form of resistance to publish-or-perish hiring, tenure, and promotion practices, or relational accounting practices that intentionally disrupt calculative audits (see Clegg et al., 2020, for some additional discussion of these practices). Such forms of resistance create the temporal and material space to dwell more in our particular places and attend to the moral duties we find there.

Summing Up

In this chapter, I have argued that scientific justification requires a committed research praxis, one where we attend to the moral and epistemic commitments that justify our work as researchers. I have described how researchers can do this by asking questions together in a place. That is, we can subject our work to insistent moral attention through collective and locally situated forms of reflection and responsibility. These forms could include reflexivity, transparency, participatory and community-oriented research practices, political, historical, and material analyses of our research traditions and products, resistance to over-generalized and "scaled" forms of neoliberal management, and other practices that help us anchor our research work to the local and communal commitments that justify it.

PART III

Charting the Moral Geography of Psychological Research

My argument so far has been that the scientistic, objectivist, and instrumentalist view of science displaces research from its real moral context and thus not only misrepresents the activities of research but, more importantly, can compromise our capacity as psychological researchers to fulfill the responsibilities inherent in our work. I have suggested a different view of science, one that takes scientific activity to be a fundamentally moral and hermeneutic endeavor; one where various social constraints and processes frame a narrative and persuasive activity, defined by a texture of personal, relational, and institutional commitments.

In addition, I have claimed that, given the moral architecture of research practices and institutions, the *justification* of science is also a primarily social and moral endeavor. Justification, I have argued, is the task of articulating the collective values underwriting the products and claims of particular research communities, evaluating the degree to which particular instances of research work reflect those values, and collectively refining the disciplinary structures, interpersonal practices, and local commitments that enact those values. I have, drawing on thinkers like Helen Longino, Lisa Osbeck, Emmanuel Levinas, and others, suggested that justification requires at least two central ideal practices: (1) an open disciplinary politics, characterized by an epistemic citizenship aimed at institutionalizing practices that challenge the status quo (particularly as a reflection of ingrained social privilege) and that foment critical discourse among the broadest possible range of interlocutors; and (2) a committed research praxis, where psychologists build into their ways of conducting research an insistent, collective, and locally situated moral critique and refinement of their research practices and traditions (for example, by asking questions together in a place).

This moral and political work, I am saying, *is* science, and this is what we should center in the teaching, reporting, and oversight of

psychological research. In Part III of this book, I provide an example of
the kind of moral attention that I have suggested is indispensable to
scientific justification, focusing on the everyday practices of psychological research. Part III is an attempt to explicate some of the various
moral affordances (i.e., the moral questions, dilemmas, and duties) of
everyday psychological research work and to reflect on the kinds of
moral questions that might help us expose and refine the commitments
underwriting that work. I approach this task in an intentionally personal and reflective way, reasoning from my own experiences as a
researcher (and mentor) and according to my own sense of what
matters or is morally justifiable. This reading of the dilemmas and
duties of psychological research is thus inevitably unique – *personal*,
as Polanyi might say – and so reflects, not a universal set of norms for
"good" science, but a particular example of moral attention to the
practices of psychological inquiry. I don't stake any irrevocable claims
on the moral interpretations that follow; I insist only on the centrality
to scientific justification of the moral attention itself.

Each of the chapters in Part III will consider one major episode in a
typical research narrative;[1] in order, these are: domain and theory
choice (Chapter 8); design and execution of research (Chapter 9);
and the interpretation and reporting of research (Chapter 10). These
divisions are intentionally conventional, as this provides an anchor
point for comparing this analysis with more familiar accounts of the
research process. In practice, all of these episodes blur into one
another, but working within this familiar structure is a useful heuristic
for orienting ourselves amidst the complex and often uncharted moral
geographies of psychological research.

This orientation within a moral geography is the primary work of
each chapter in Part III. I take up that work in terms of the moral
choices, interpersonal relationships, and institutional structures that, it
seems to me, we must attend to in each phase of research. I choose
these points of focus because, in my view, they house the most important moral affordances of research work. It is when I am faced with
moral questions or dilemmas that I must articulate, or at least enact,
my values; when I enter into relationships, I enter into moral obligations to others (e.g., to be kind or honest); when I navigate institutions

---

[1] No doubt this story can be told in many ways, but I hope most psychological
researchers will be able to recognize what they do in this rendering.

(universities, review boards, journals, etc.), I am navigating shared norms, rules, requirements, and so on.

What I hope to make clear in this consideration of moral choices, interpersonal relationships, and institutional structures are not just our moral responsibilities within research, but also the inseparability of those responsibilities from the proper conduct of science. I conclude each of these chapters with a set of possible questions that the members of any research community might ask themselves (or have addressed to them); these, I hope, provide at least a starting place for the collective moral attention that, I have argued, anchors the justification of psychological research.

8 | *Domain and Theory Choice*

Research has to start somewhere and often enough it is in uncertainty: an undergraduate looking for "lab experience"; a doctoral candidate hoping to conjure up a dissertation; a novice researcher looking to "break in" to some domain; or even an experienced researcher puzzling over the next question or trying out new waters. A buffet of possible "topics" confronts the questing researcher and a riot of theories to explain them.

But there is something (sometimes cruelly) deceptive about the notion of "choosing a research topic." Deceptive not just because topics are often assigned rather than chosen, but also because the notion of "topic" obscures what is really involved in becoming socialized to some research domain. To do research of a certain kind is not just to choose some domain of interest; it is to choose a community, a set of norms and traditions, a set of canonical theories and methods (and other practices), a whole way of looking at the world. And these "choices" are often so constrained – by the requirements of instructors, advisers, supervisors, employers, institutions, review boards, disciplinary conventions, and so on – that they don't always feel entirely agentic (particularly for those with less institutional influence).

Still, these choices, such as they are, are the entry points into research and they represent a first moral stand on what research (and science) should be like. That stand may be more like a confused tumble into something we don't fully understand,[1] but we are still responsible for it however we come to it. What is at stake in that stand, what it claims for us, is an endorsement of a particular community and its ways of seeing and interacting with the world. In choosing a research domain, we are choosing to contribute to the ideas and practices of that community, to build relationships with the real people who make up that community, and to accept (at least some) responsibility for the political

---

[1] A description that doesn't necessarily only apply to novice researchers.

practices of that community. In the remainder of this chapter, I'll describe each of these commitments in turn, along with a discussion of the moral affordances and dilemmas they inscribe.

Making a Contribution (Becoming Socialized)

Contributing to a scholarly community means not just sharing some interests; it means conforming our questions and problem frames to a language that the community will understand. Theory choice is thus not simply a rational selection of the "best" theory from an infinite range of possible theories (or even just our best ideas about how to explain something); it is always one turn in an ongoing conversation and so must conform to the language and structure of that conversation. The possibilities for framing a hearable theory or research question are always finite and historically dependent. Abraham Maslow's attempts to convince mainstream experimental journals to print his work on peak experiences is a good example of this point. For years, he tried and failed; but he wasn't asking the questions that others were asking and he wasn't asking them in the same ways that others were (using the same methods, making the same assumptions about science, etc.). In the end, he had to try to start a new conversation, and what he had to say was never really quite heard (see Head, Quigua, and Clegg, 2019 for a more complete discussion).

Choices about domain or theory are thus less like a solitary imagination of nature's workings and more like an uncertain and contentious conversation; picture not the lonely man of science but the (mostly) friendly scrum of the lab meeting.[2] Research theories, questions, and ideas reside in geographically and temporally distributed exchanges and to contribute to science is to take up residence within these exchanges; to learn to see and treat the world and the people in it as the terms of the conversation allow. And these terms are never morally neutral; particularly in psychology, as here they will always bear on how we see and treat persons (as agents or objects, as bodies or persons, etc.). Psychological theories and traditions are never innocent; they plot people in the world and concrete consequences often follow. A woman's right to vote, own property, or resist violence have all been materially impacted by how psychology plotted them (as sexual

---

[2] Depending on the lab.

objects, as neutered men, etc.); members of the LGBTQ community have suffered generations of abusive "treatment" because of a psychology that plotted them as diseased; it is still legal in the USA to forcibly sterilize the "disabled" because of a psychology that plots particular persons as "imbeciles" (see Chapters 3–6). These historical traditions of research were not politically or morally neutral and neither are those we choose now. By contributing to particular communities or working with particular theories, by accepting the terms of these communities, we are choosing the commitments that come with them (or perhaps challenging them, a question I will return to in the last part of this chapter).

At least as important as the ideas are the practices that we import from any community to which we contribute. Ways of working are just as constrained by tradition as are ways of thinking. I recall, for example, once submitting an article to a journal where all of the reviewers made it clear that studies not employing eye-tracking software were simply not the right sort. Both narrow (e.g., the decision by the journal *Basic and Applied Social Psychology* to reject any studies using Null Hypothesis Significance Testing; see Trafimow and Marks, 2016) and broad (e.g., the historical disinclination among mainstream journals to publish qualitative research) constrictions of acceptable practice are common across psychology. Thus, choosing to contribute to some disciplinary conversation is also a commitment to certain kinds of practice and, just like ideas, practices all have moral valences. Different research practices commit us to (or against), for example, deception, value neutrality, feminism, determinism, self-disclosure, emotional distance, and countless other value orientations. Domain and theory choice are thus also choices about the kinds of work and the kinds of relationships we want in our research lives. If I want to contribute to experimental social psychology, I should probably be ready to lie (or at least mislead); if I want to contribute to neuroanatomy or physiology, I should probably be ready to kill (or at least to work among the dead); if I want to contribute to research in high-security settings (prisons, hospitals, etc.), I should probably be ready to subdue (or ask others to do so on my behalf).

Many of our moral quandaries as a discipline are folded into these seemingly neutral choices around what to study and how. When researchers in the late nineteenth and early twentieth centuries chose to contribute to research on race differences, they were choosing, whether wittingly or no, to build the ideas and contribute to the projects of a eugenicist elite. When researchers working with immigrant communities chose to administer standardized intelligence tests, they were choosing to feed anti-immigrant and protectionist ideologies. And, though it will not be easy to see from the muddle of the present, researchers are making the same kinds of choices now. My "choice" of a "research topic," practice, or theory is always a moral and political commitment.

Building a Scientific Community (Building Trust and Good Faith)

The choice of a community to which we will contribute is not only about ideas or practices; it is also about the people with whom we will work, will critique and be critiqued by, will share meals and hotel rooms with. Science is, most fundamentally, a delicate human system, a network of relationships, all of which require a great deal of trust (see Part II). No one researcher can verify the results of every other, and so we must trust that other researchers employ appropriate practices, make responsible and warrantable interpretations, report honestly, and so on. Indeed, even within a single study, the process and outcomes of research depend on the good faith of a whole network of contributors – collaborators, administrative and technical staff, participants, reviewers, and so on. It is perhaps trivial to point out that even a little bit of bad faith – like analysts who fudge data, lab workers with loose or improperly documented procedures, or participants who deceive – is sufficient to compromise the integrity and usefulness of a study (and of science).

The activities of science, in other words, are distributed among actual persons and this means that the most common and the most indispensable epistemic act in science is to trust in the good faith of other people. And this also means that trust in the good faith of our community is, by a vast and insurmountable margin, the primary warrant behind all scientific claims. Without it, nothing else we do in science matters.[3]

---

[3] I suspect that to some this statement will seem controversial, but I don't think it is. Imagine a science where every data point might be an intentional misrepresentation, every claim a fabrication; what would good experimental design or cutting-edge analytic procedures matter?

This trust and good faith are what we give to a research community and what we expect in return, but these extend well beyond strictly epistemic considerations. We trust that members of our community will negotiate funding, collaboration, and credit in good faith; we trust that they will not intentionally harm others or knowingly contribute to exploitation, violence, oppression, discrimination, or other unconscionable acts; we trust that they will be collegial at meetings and respectful of others' work; we trust that they will not engage in exploitative, harassing, or aggressive behavior toward other members of our community. In short, we are trusting others to act in good faith and so make the kind of community where trust, and thus science, is possible.

Building this community of trust is mostly a matter of attending to particular relationships and acting within them in good faith – small histories of reliable, competent, professional, and honest interactions in study trials, lab meetings, conferences, manuscript reviews, and so on constitute the foundations of trust that undergird a research community. In some communities, scandals over falsified data and failed replications, as well as long-standing questions about the mistreatment of research subjects, have tended to undermine those foundations, sowing doubt about the legitimacy of research (see Parts I and II for a discussion of these issues). Smaller dishonesties or cruelties are less visible but have the same kinds of effects. The sloppy assistant or checked-out participant will probably never be seen or known, but these too undermine science.

If acting in bad faith can undermine the trust that founds good science, then acting in good faith can surely help to repair it. In research, we participate in a whole array of relationships that require our good faith, but our relationships with those who mentor or influence our entry into a research community are probably those most germane to questions of domain and theory choice. Most often, these are advisors, supervisors, or experienced colleagues; but sometimes these are people we may not know but whose work guides our ideas and practices. These relationships involve reciprocal, though usually hierarchical, dependencies. One of my mentors in graduate school, for example, oversaw a modest publishing empire, and so he needed reliable editorial help from his students. Some of us did administrative work for pay or credit; some reviewed submissions or occasionally wrote commentaries or book chapters; the most advanced (including those post-degree) published their own edited volumes or edited special issues of journals. This whole network depended on a feeling of fair treatment and non-exploitation, a sense that opportunities to make money or publish offset the labor involved. It also depended on mutual commitments to high scholarly standards, a great deal of collaboration and support, and general good will.

The good faith within this community was carefully nurtured, and this is, I think, a pretty basic duty for scientists. Researchers depend upon and have to trust one another, and in the graded hierarchies by which we enter into a research community, special attention to unequal power, access, and resources is a part of that duty. When we choose to contribute to some research community, we are choosing to be beginners, to need mentors, to pay our dues (which usually means working harder and being rewarded less). When we occupy more influential positions within research communities, we are choosing to arbitrate resources, access, and rewards and so are also taking on the responsibility to act fairly, honestly, and in the best interests of our community. All of these relationships (with all their tensions and potentials for abuse) can work in an atmosphere of good faith; and they can be strained or even fail under conditions of exploitation, deception, incompetence, or harm. Holding this all together by our good faith attention to particular relationships and persons is among our most vital "contributions" to some domain or tradition of research.

Transforming Research Communities (Epistemic Citizenship)

Though domain and theory choices are choices of habitus, worldview, and community, they do not preclude resistance and intentional change. Quite the reverse: citizenship in any community entails the basic civic duty of working toward the best possible shared practices, and this can mean working against prevailing assumptions, commitments, methods, theories, and so on.

Though obviously controversial, the Reproducibility Project (Nosek, Aarts, Anderson, Kappes, and Open Science Collaboration, 2015) is an interesting example of an attempt to transform the political structure of a research community. The problem of too few replications in psychology is pretty universally acknowledged, but the reward structures of research are such that replication is discouraged, and so little has been done to address this issue (Clegg, Wiggins, and Ostenson, 2020). The

Open Science Collaboration took a rather direct approach to the problem by creating a structure for conducting regular replications. Not at all surprisingly, this inspired some resistance. The status quo always resists change (though not always for bad reasons), and in this case there were all sorts of political and structural reasons why change might be undesirable. Publication and citation are the primary coins of the research realm, proxies for credibility and gateways to influence, and a push toward replication threatens both existing publications and the workflow of future ones. Nobody wants their research delegitimized, of course, and some "targets" of replication raised a fuss. Pressure toward replication is also a sort of "existential" threat because journals hardly ever publish straight replications (mostly because of the constant drive for novelty), and researchers don't have time for work that won't be published (or that will be difficult to publish, particularly in more prestigious outlets). The political structure of research in psychology involves fairly standard neoliberal practices – commoditized publication, hyper-competitive submission and rejection practices, measurement (in the form of citation indices and impact factors), and surveillance (in tenure review, for example) – and these all militate against the slower, more careful culture of replication (see Ostenson, Clegg, and Wiggins, 2017).

Structural and political realities of this sort constrain and shape the scientific process and so part of doing science responsibly is to attend to and refine our political practices (e.g., most seem to agree that we need to replicate more and better, but that won't be possible until we engage with and challenge the political structures that prevent it). Responsible participation in a research community or contribution to some tradition of theory thus entails some understanding of the historical and political structures of these communities and traditions, both because these tell us what kinds of commitments we are making but also what (and perhaps whether) change is possible. We don't just do research in laboratories or on computers, but in society and board meetings, through legislative sessions and policy reports, on editorial and review boards; in short, through *epistemic citizenship* (see Chapter 6). When we are orienting ourselves toward some new program of research, when we are deciding what it will be, what theories and traditions it will invoke and participate in, what communities it will speak to, how it will plot particular persons in moral and political space, our best intentions can come to nothing if we don't also strive to understand such institutional practices, their histories and their consequences, and to act responsibly within them (including acting to change them).

Some Questions

My aim in this chapter was to plot the moral geography of domain and theory choice and no doubt I did it idiosyncratically and imperfectly, but I won't feel too bad if I at least did enough to show that this terrain is, in fact, moral and political; and I hope this encourages us to ask different kinds of questions about what we choose to study. To be clear, I am not discounting the importance of the questions we might usually ask ourselves when setting out to do research; questions like: *What am I interested in? What is important to me? What kind of work would I like to do? What kind of work am I good at? What will be useful to me in my career? What mentors are available and what kind of work do they do? What are important questions or problems for the field or for society in general? What theories make the most sense of my questions? What theories are the strongest, most endorsed, or most well-supported?*

These are important questions, but too narrow to address the broader human context of research. I hope to have raised additional questions that more fully express the scope of relevant concerns. I hope we will also ask questions like: *How have the research traditions I participate in been (or could be) deployed politically? What acts have they been used to justify? What ideologies do they draw on or support? How have they contributed to (or could they contribute to) injustice, exploitation, discrimination, harm, or other acts inconsistent with what I (and my communities) value? What practices do they support or discourage (or have been deployed to support or discourage)? How do these practices treat persons and places? Are these practices honest, benevolent, just, and otherwise consistent with what I (and my communities) value? What are the history and culture of these practices and what other traditions have contributed to them? How do the theories I deploy frame others? What kinds of persons (or other beings) do they imagine, allow, exclude, demean, valorize, or pathologize? What values do they inscribe or undermine? Who are the people who make up the research communities to which I contribute? What are their (and my) norms, expectations, and values? How do they (and I) treat others? Are they (and am I) honest, responsible, fair, collegial, and decent? Do they (and do I) act in good faith? How do the institutional or administrative structures of the traditions to which I wish to contribute constrain my work? Do these require me to do things inconsistent with my values (epistemic or otherwise)? Do these structures discriminate, obstruct, misrepresent, or harm? Have they done so in the past or could they do so in the future? How can I act responsibly within them? How can I act to change them?*

Questions like those in the first set will perhaps aim us toward interesting, useful, important, even lucrative research; but questions like those in the second set can lead us toward *good* research.

9 | *The Design and Conduct of Research*

Research must take some form or other, and we generally call figuring that out "design," though as we've already seen, participation in a research community constrains and predefines the acceptable range of design choices. Design, like domain and theory choice, happens within a preexisting moral geography and so must be responsive to a whole range of political commitments and social institutions. "Design," in other words, may again be a somewhat misleading word, implying as it does a fully intentional, agentic, and individually determined plan, rather than the more relational and political negotiations that actually determine research. In research, as Kurt Danziger (1990) argues, "both the immediate investigative situation and the research community are ... embedded in social relationships that extend beyond them" (p. 7), and these relationships, as well as the research produced within them, mutually shape one another.

In *Constructing the Subject*, his landmark historical analysis of psychological research, Danziger (1990) provides a compelling analysis of the social contexts of research. One of his most telling case studies is of "experiments" in the nineteenth-century French clinical tradition. According to Danziger, these "emerged in a medical context" where "those who functioned as subjects ... were identified by labels such as 'hysterics' or 'somnambulists'" (p. 53). Thus the "essential features" of the "physician patient relationship ... were simply continued into the experimental situation" (p. 53). Research was conducted on "medically stigmatized" (p. 55) "subjects" (a term with a medical origin, referring originally to corpses used in dissection) who "underwent or suffered" (p. 53) experimental manipulation, and played "the role of a biological organism or medical preparation" (p. 62).

This arrangement was quite clearly an extension of the social and institutional relationships of those involved as well as an expression of the values, needs, and commitments of the dominant group

100

(physicians/experimenters). This "shaping" of research "design" also traveled in the other direction, research practices coming to shape life outside of the laboratory. These experiments relied on "a glaring status difference between ... male scientists and their generally female lay subjects" (Danziger, 1990, p. 53), and this was reflected in an investigator attitude that "does not think of the subject as a human agent but simply as material for the demonstration of his pet ideas" (p. 62). This instrumental and exploitative attitude traveled into other contexts, most famously in "Charcot's notorious public demonstrations of hysteria at the Salpetriere" (p. 62), demonstrations where "hysterical" patients were required to perform in weekly shows, submit to public hypnotism and demonstrate symptoms like catalepsy, somnambulism, and seizures (among other "tricks").

Danziger's analysis is historically specific, but the kind of social embeddedness described is common to all research. None who design and conduct research can escape their own moral and political positioning. Of course, this does not mean that we can't shape the larger social order and our place within it. In fact, doing research is one of the most significant ways that a psychologist can shape the larger social order. Research creates its own micro-culture – particular kinds of relationships, ways of speaking, ways of defining problems or success, ways of working in spaces, with people, with power – and this micro-culture travels. We see this in Danziger's analysis, as both exploitation and social control flowed out of the laboratory and into medical and educational contexts. When we are designing research, we are thus engaging in a negotiation about the kind of world we want to live in, the kinds of practices we want to transmit to the larger culture we inhabit. Perhaps more than anything else, this is the moral burden of research *design* – to take responsibility for the kinds of social forces that we invite (or perhaps decline to resist) into how we design and conduct research and, even more importantly, for the ways that our design choices then structure (or have the potential to structure) institutions, politics, and persons.

The remainder of this chapter will be devoted to explicating how particular choices about the design and conduct of research raise these (and other) moral questions. But before I proceed, let me say a few words about my admittedly idiosyncratic use of the word "design." Typically, research design is presented as an entirely epistemic concern – that is, as a matter of choosing data collection procedures that will provide valid answers to certain kinds of questions. These procedures come in *kinds* (experimental, quasi-experimental, cross-sectional, etc.), with most methods texts spending most of their time naming and describing these, demarcating their best practices, and plotting them within an evidentiary hierarchy. I will make no use of these conventions for several reasons. First, nearly every methods text in psychology will do so competently and so the ground is more than adequately covered. Second, these heuristic divisions do little to distinguish the various moral affordances of research design and so are of no particular help in my task here. Finally, and most importantly, the epistemic concerns that drive these distinctions are, to speak frankly, insignificant in comparison with the moral questions that concern us here. If what we do in research is cruel, unjust, deceptive, or oppressive (or complicit in these or other moral failings), then it hardly matters whether we employ a Solomon Four Group or a Non-Equivalent Control Groups Design.

My questions here, then, are not about design kinds, nor their putative epistemic affordances. I am concerned, rather, with how we actually produce the practical activities that constitute research, the dilemmas and duties these activities inscribe, as well as the relational and civic responsibilities they entail. In the process, I will be troubling perfectly ordinary things, but not in a perverse or precious way (i.e., not "just for the fun of it"). My aim is just to "see" (and show) the ordinary activities of research, but the ordinary is often the most invisible and, when we look at it closely, can become quite strange. I again make use of fairly conventional distinctions to structure these considerations, focusing, in turn, on research funding, space, equipment, organization, and participation.

Funding (Resources)

Research funds (or resources) come with conditions but, in some form or another (a grant, a professor's salary, an individual sacrifice of time), they are necessary for research. This dynamic plots a political struggle within every research project (though we may not always notice it). Research requires resources and where these come from and how they are disposed shapes that research, often in ways that run counter, or at least oblique, to the epistemic aims of research or to the personal commitments of researchers. To do research is to take up this struggle between what we might like (or feel compelled) to do ideally and what the available resources permit.

Funding, and resources more generally, can constrain in a variety of ways. The simplest (and probably most familiar) are the limitations entailed in having space, time, and money insufficient to our ideal design. I recall, for example, an institutional evaluation project where our ideal design would have involved hundreds of interviews. But there were only a few of us and no funds to pay more; we had a limited timeframe with no opportunity to extend the study; and the institutional actors were unwilling to all be interviewed anyway. So, we modified the design (using targeted interviews and focus groups, some online data collection, etc.) until it fit within the available resources. Design always involves practical negotiations of these kinds, and these will carry moral implications. In our design modifications, for example, we undoubtedly made some stories invisible and we had to consider whom we might have silenced.

There are also more subtle ways that the available resources can constrain or pattern how we do research. Most research in psychology, for example, generalizes from the experiences of psychology undergraduates, and most of these come from the so-called WEIRD (Western, educated, industrialized, rich, and democratic; Henrich, Heine, and Norenzayan, 2010) demographic. There is thus no question that choosing the convenience of studying our own students has produced a psychology (both ideologically and in terms of its practices) where the concerns, values, worldviews, and psychologies of the world's dominant social groups are grossly over-represented; and, of course, these values are exported and imposed in the form of ethnocentric self-report measures, standardized tests, diagnostic systems, treatments, and so on. In this way, the whole discipline of psychology has been profoundly patterned by a particular resource availability issue. These small choices, these seemingly very local resource negotiations, can thus have far-reaching social and political consequences.

Perhaps the most visible and immediate resource conditions are those that come with direct funding or resources (grant funding, donated facilities, awards or appointments, consulting fees, etc.). Such conditions can be explicit – like grant requirements that research concern a certain topic, address a certain problem, or employ a certain methodology – or implicit – like the subtle pressures to serve company interests that come with corporate-funded research. The 1911 research on the cognitive effects of caffeine, conducted by Harry and Leta Hollingworth, is an interesting example of such pressures. That research was commissioned by Coca Cola ahead of a Supreme Court trial considering whether caffeine could be considered an "adulterated" beverage, and Harry Hollingworth was asked to assess the cognitive effects of caffeine (including whether it disturbed sleep or was habit-forming). There is no evidence, nor reason to assume, that this research was explicitly biased by its corporate sponsorship (in fact, it was a model of careful research design); yet, the findings suggested that caffeine produced positive cognitive effects without any serious negative side-effects (see Benjamin, 2003, for a more complete discussion of this episode).

These kinds of financial forces can shape not only a particular study, but whole disciplines. A good example is the barrage of focused funding aimed at genetic and other biological markers of mental health characterizing the NIMH during Thomas Insel's tenure at its head (2002–2015). Although Insel himself acknowledged that this effort largely failed to improve the lives of those diagnosed with mental illness (Rogers, 2017), it still produced a strong multidisciplinary push toward research into biologically oriented diagnosis and treatment of mental illness.

There is likely nothing surprising in these examples. Obviously, it must be true that those who "fund" research, even if it is only a university paying a faculty salary, shape the kind of research that can be done, and every researcher must negotiate the compromises inherent in that funding dynamic. There may be no clear way beyond the tensions and compromises produced in such a dynamic, but we can still turn our moral attention to their consequences; we can consider both how our decisions about funding impact real persons and how they help to shape whose interests and values dominate the discipline.

Space (Dwelling)

Research also requires space[1] and space carries its own moral affordances. If research design is a matter of making the kind of world we want to live in, then how we work with space is a matter of making the kind of home we want to inhabit; or, perhaps more precisely (and to

---

[1] Though in many fields, this space is increasingly digital.

borrow Heidegger's, 1993, term), the kind of *dwelling* we want to *do*. We probably generally think of "research space" as a set of Cartesian coordinates (usually a grayish box on a campus somewhere) with room for equipment and/or people performing procedures; sometimes that space is not "mine," but a space in the "real world" (often a different grayish box at a clinic, state agency, school, etc.); sometimes that space is distributed through an ether of hard and soft networks (e.g., Mechanical Turk). However it is configured, we can't adequately account for that space unless we understand it not just as a metric volume, but as something we make and do, something constituted through practices of dwelling.

The iconic Stanford Prison Study (Haney, Banks, and Zimbardo, 1973) is an interesting example of my point here. The space where the "prison" was built was really just a basement with some small rooms, not so different from any research "lab." What made that space a prison weren't its dimensions, but the forms of dwelling involved in the study. The space was made bare and institutional, with somber colors, simple and straight lines, depersonalized and uninviting. Doors were locked and only some participants had the keys, and these engaged in surveillance, bullying, coercion, and domination. Everyone was watched and control became the primary form of dwelling, even for Phillip Zimbardo, the director of the study. The nature of the study and its meaning were bound up in, constituted by, these forms of dwelling. Without understanding them, we understand almost nothing about the space or even the study itself.

This is an admittedly extreme case, where space and dwelling were more determinative of research than might be the case in other studies; but extreme cases can help us see more clearly the dimensions of the question. The degree may be different, but in every study, our practices of dwelling are community practices; they are forms of hospitality (or hostility) toward others and of conservation (or consumption) of shared resources and places.

"Research space" is thus perhaps better understood as a form of collective dwelling, where the good will (cooperation, courtesy, community) of all involved determines the character of the research. Every study passes through the hands of a whole village – grant reviewers and staff, review boards, department administrative personnel, building security, collaborators, post-docs, students, participants, and so on – and each study depends not just on the honesty of all these actors, but on their willingness to be helpful, to make many small (and sometimes large) sacrifices of time, on their willingness to think the best of, and offer their best intentions to, a project (from which many of them will receive very little benefit). For many years, for example, my students and I had the help of a very conscientious IRB manager; she would remind us about deadlines, review every proposal before submission (and usually help us rewrite it), advocate for us with the review board, expedite time-sensitive amendments, and generally make pretty effortless one of the least enjoyable aspects of research. Her conscientious good will was a significant contribution to the flourishing of our research.

In research, then, responsible dwelling is, at least in part, about the arts of hospitality, courtesy, and community. These make (or mar) the spaces we share. Part of our moral labor, part of doing good science, is thus an attention to the often invisible communities that support research and to the practices that either foster or interfere with the good will that nourishes such communities (and, through them, science). We can't hope to be exploitative, arrogant, dismissive, ungrateful, graceless, demanding, or entitled and still expect a flourishing (in the fullest sense of that term) research enterprise.

The demands of *conservation* are another way that research dwelling can carry moral affordances. We generally speak of conservation in the context of the sustainable use of natural spaces or resources, and that is part of what I mean here. It is certainly a general duty among all researchers to create, contribute to, or advocate for, research spaces that are not destructive or exploitative of our shared natural environment; spaces that are healthy for those who inhabit them and practices that conserve and nourish healthy spaces. But my meaning is broader than this; I am speaking also about conserving and sustaining our shared social, moral, and communal geographies. A research space is sustainable in this broader sense when our practices don't destroy or compromise our capacity to do research – for example, when we don't alienate the community or organization where we do our research, or we don't exhaust or exploit our research assistants – and when these nourish the community and participation that make research possible. Conservation is thus a matter of creating research spaces that don't simply consume resources in an instrumental drive for productivity, but that participate in the places and communities they inhabit, drawing from them but also giving back to them in ways that strengthen ties and increase our capacity to work there, that fertilize and cross-fertilize in an organic (rather than industrial) kind of growth.

The classic Marienthal study (Jahoda, Lazarsfeld, and Zeisel, 2002), conducted in 1930s Austria, illustrates some of what I am saying here. The study itself was occasioned by a fairly typical story of industrialized production – a large factory town destroyed when the national banking system collapsed and the factory was forced to close. The researchers, intending to study the effects of long-term unemployment, first built ties with the community, living there for periods of time and participating in community life. They eventually came to feel an attachment and care for the community, organizing an ambulance service, clothing distributions, sewing and gymnastics classes, advocating for the community politically (even years later), and generally trying to participate in sustaining what they called "the weary community." They did all of this at least partly from humanity, but it also made possible research of a very intimate kind; research that produced deep insights and that aided the community members to survive. This is a striking case of conservation practices on the part of researchers – practices that nourished the community, which in turn nourished the research.

The Marienthal (Jahoda et al., 2002) study is also an interesting example of how a research "space," and our dwelling within it, can require attention to structural, institutional, and political questions. The researchers couldn't simply do nothing more than ask their questions or take their notes and still be responsible, effective researchers. To be effective (and also just decent), they had to build ties with and care for the community, and that sometimes meant political advocacy. Years after the study, for example, Marie Jahoda advocated on behalf of the people of Marienthal (against her own politics, in fact) for a welfare-to-work project because she considered it the only way to counter the resignation of community members.

Though this account of research space is undoubtedly unusual, I think it will still be recognizable to researchers. Most of us have learned from experience that hospitality, courtesy, and good will can make our research "homes" places to live and work well in, and that care for, rather than simply making use of, these research spaces (both physical and social), can make them places that nourish and last.

Equipment (Embodiment)

Much like space, research equipment is something familiar that becomes more complex (and strange) upon inspection. We generally think of equipment in terms of the tools that occupy "labs" but these tools are simply a special case of a larger category of *augmentations*. What makes them tools is not their shape but the way we use them to extend our capabilities; the way we extend, or augment, our embodiment through them. Martin Heidegger (1962), for example, spoke of the hammer that extends my hand and Donna Haraway (1987) of the "cyborg" embodied, and extended, through digital machinery and distributed networks. When we use tools, we feel (the vibrations of the hammer) and think (the "links" of the web) through them and so make them part of ourselves. To use equipment is, in a very basic sense, to become grafted to that equipment, to reorder our lives, bodies, and communities to their shapes (and change their shapes to fit our bodies).

The question of what "equipment" to use is thus a question about whether and in what ways we are willing to transform and extend our individual and collective embodiment. Such considerations likely seem morally insignificant in most cases. Few of us will have to consider whether our conscience permits the use of shock-plates (Seligman), orphans (Watson), staged heart-attacks (Milgram), or live rat behead-ings (Landis) as "equipment." We are more likely to make decisions like what kinds of video equipment to use; whether to do paper or online data collection; or whether scaled self-reports will work for our study. These seem like much more comfortable kinds of decisions; not even moral really, but purely technical or instrumental.

But if we understand these kinds of decisions as contributing to new forms of embodiment, then even seemingly insignificant decisions take on moral import. Consider, for example, the decision to use scaled self-report measures. These are surely the most common kind of equipment in psychology; a seemingly uncontroversial default data collection method. But they are not just a means of collecting data; they have become ubiquitous elements of modern culture, repatterning how we experience our world. Even very small children now learn to imagine themselves in ranked increments,[2] to take "quizzes," "inventories," "tests," or "surveys" that will tell them about their personality, voca-tion, mate, or disorder. It is not an exaggeration to say that this continual use of self-reports has transformed bodies, consciousness, and culture: we now learn to see and scan horizontal arrays of

[2] All of us born, it seems, in intervals of 5, 7, or 9.

incrementing numerals as ratings; to circle, fill in, click, or tap serial ratings; to examine ourselves in an abstracted third person; to imagine ourselves and others as various parts measurable. Because self-reports are all around us, they draw us into their forms of imagination and practice and extend us in particular ways – specifically, as self-rating, self-scaling, self-surveilling subjects, a form of embodiment of dubious utility to you or me, but an obvious boon in the sorting and ordering of populations.

My point here is that equipment has its own affordances and these are not morally neutral, neither in their histories nor in the current forms of embodiment that they make possible. Just as research design is a broad commitment to a certain way of structuring the world and space a commitment to forms of dwelling in it, choices about equipment are commitments to ways of being embodied in that space and world; and, crucially, to the kinds of embodiment we impose on others. It is, I would contend, wantonly irresponsible to imagine such commitments in purely instrumental terms – in terms of what equipment will produce data easiest to collect or analyze, what equipment will be cheapest or will fit the lab space, or even what equipment will produce the most effective or predictable manipulations. Without considering also what we are asking others (and ourselves) to take into their (and our) bodies and how this might pattern their (and our) lives, such considerations can easily become exploitative or even harmful. We will be able to see more clearly the moral costs of these seemingly simple choices when we ask questions about not just how equipment might be useful, but about how it makes new ways of being embodied in the world – questions like "Do I want to live in a world where we make machines to shock dogs into despondency?" or "Would I ask my grandmother to behead a rat?" or "Would I want my child to live in a society that requires her to put herself under constant surveillance?"

As in previous sections, I am speaking here of choices, but it is important to always keep in view the ways that external forces limit what choices are possible. I mentioned in an earlier example how practical considerations led me and my co-researchers to the use of digital and networked forms of equipment, even though these were not our ideal design. Similarly, I see students consistently choosing research designs that are simple, quick, cost-effective, and light on labor because these are their constraints. Sometimes equipment seems to choose us, rather than we it (I might use equipment that my institution already has or services that it already pays for; I might use the kinds of equipment everybody else uses, etc.).

One constraint that seems to particularly structure equipment use is the requirement that research be "scalable" within some form of institutional management. Research on teaching and learning, for example, is mostly aimed at "improving outcomes" in an assessment context; likewise, clinical research focuses mostly on treatment outcomes under the scrutiny of third-party payers. We live amid a kind of neoliberal numerology that demands equipment capable of abstracting, scaling, and instrumentalizing the ends of research (and practice). As I have said, such pressures cannot be effectively met without participation in the larger political commons. My best, most thoughtful uses of equipment – uses that reflect careful, responsible, far-sighted research craft – may only languish without support or credence if the only available intellectual spaces are dominated by the heedless instrumentalities of a managerial culture.

Organization

Even the simplest research requires a community and that community must be organized in some way or another. Research involves countless decisions and interactions, a continual coordination of tasks and schedules, and how this is all ordered amounts to a small, local culture. Some research takes place in large and complex lab collectives where the culture is not so small or simple, while other projects involve only one primary researcher whose community consists only of the minimal professional networks necessary to publish research (e.g., colleagues who provide resources, subjects review, journal review and editorial, and associated administrative support). Regardless of the complexity involved, researchers must make choices about planning, governance, and relational practice, and these are all basically moral choices.

Planning is fairly universal to all kinds and complexities of research, though, of course, not everyone plans well or wisely.[3] In any case, some order is demanded and how it is provided carries important moral affordances. These affordances are perhaps not immediately obvious, as planning can seem like the most perfectly instrumental of

---

[3] I, myself, have had to sometimes contend with an unfortunate inclination toward "winging it."

activities; simply a matter of getting everything done in the right order and on time. But how we order activities within a particular time-scale is (to repeat my refrain) far from morally neutral.

I have already alluded to the neoliberal structuring of research settings and this is perhaps the best example of how our time-scales can have moral significance. As Sugarman and Thrift (2017) have noted, a neoliberal time-scale is one of continual acceleration (i.e., more and more pressed for time), demanding internalized commitments to competition, efficiency, and productivity. These are all essentially institutional commitments, commitments to the effective functioning of bureaucratic systems, to the production and maintenance of growth, resources, and power, and to the instrumentalization of persons and places to these larger institutional ends. It is not hard to recognize this sort of time-scale in research planning; that planning is often organized around institutional deadlines (for grants, review cycles, revisions, etc.), oriented toward rapid production (i.e., publish or perish), and plots persons and places in terms of efficiency and productivity (e.g., maximizing the number of subjects or the amount of time in a research lab).

I suspect that to most researchers these commitments don't feel like commitments at all, but simply the necessities of planning a complex activity with limited time and resources. The neoliberal time-scale has become thoroughly "naturalized," and certainly institutionalized, in most research contexts. We may not see other ways of planning, other commitments that we could make, because every resource we might deploy, every institution we might inhabit, every disciplinary practice, is already plotted on the neoliberal time-scale and this makes any other choice seem invisible. We *could* plan with an eye to nourishing community, protecting shared spaces, or carefully incubating ideas, but from within the institutional demands we all face, these commitments can seem, at best, idealistic and, at worst, laughably naïve or even unimaginable. Here, again, citizen action in a larger political world is, at least in part, where good science must be done.[4]

---

[4] Indeed, to attend to our *personal* responsibilities in research while ignoring the neoliberal structures we inhabit is a sure way to cede those responsibilities to some kind of bureaucracy. A standard part of the neoliberal playbook is to individualize all responsibilities, transform them into "procedures," and then subject them to surveillance and enforcement (i.e., what Foucault called "governmentality").

The organization of research also entails more intimate, interpersonal kinds of responsibilities. The ordering of research activities always involves (usually many) others and so we are always choosing how we will treat them. I have written already about the honesty, courtesy, and hospitality that foster good will and good faith in these relationships, so I won't say more on those subjects. But some kinds of relationships require more than this; some require attention and care over longer periods of time. Our relationships with those who help to conduct research (collaborators, partners, students, assistants, etc.) are of this sort. My collaborations with other scholars have been the most rewarding of professional experiences, but they have all required care to flourish. These collaborations have worked when we all made efforts to show respect, patience, collegiality, and kindness (and have floundered, sometimes badly, when these duties have been ignored); when we each respected the time, external commitments, and values of others; when we acknowledged the needs of others as persons; when we strove to believe the best of others, seek accommodation, treat our differences as resources rather than struggles, and so on.

There is no way to enumerate all of the local relational practices that might create strong and flourishing collaborations, particularly as these will vary with time, person, and context; but I can argue, with Noddings (2013), Gilligan (1982), and many others, that relational care is the basic shape of these practices. We can, of course, choose to ignore the exigencies of relationship, or attend to them in exploitative, autocratic, or dismissive ways – we can, in short, choose not to care – but those exigencies remain and bear on the moral and epistemic qualities of our science. As I have said already, how we design and conduct research travels into the world, coloring both the claims we make and the practices we transmit. Charcot's exploitation and misogyny (attitudes he likely shared with a great many of his gender, time, and class) didn't just stay in the clinic or lab, but radiated out in practices and ideas.

The exigencies of care are never easily met and these are further complicated by the complex power dynamics that inhabit most research collectives. Generally speaking, collectives, and to some degree even simple collaborations, require some form of governance to deal with such dynamics. By governance, I mean the formal and informal articulation of power relationships and of procedures for arbitration, redress, and so on. Most larger research collectives have quite hierarchical power structures, but even in more lateral power structures, it is necessary to articulate how decisions will be made, conflicts arbitrated, complaints adjudicated, harms redressed, and so on. Collaborators will have different ideas about theory and design, about what questions to ask, what procedures to use, how to recruit participants, how to distribute resources and labor, how to navigate interpersonal relationships, the order of authorship, and countless other considerations. Such differences will have to be resolved in one way or another, and how we do so constitutes a sort of laboratory micro-politics. The more hierarchical a research collective, the more the responsibility for arbitrating such politics travels upward, but in all cases, all collaborators share some responsibility for the basic fairness of these political processes. Fair treatment, transparent processes, and equitable outcomes are basic conditions for functional governance, and so good research depends on meeting these and other relational exigencies.

I recall, for example, a research collaboration where a lack of transparency created some serious difficulties, ultimately creating some bad feeling and slowing the project (and perhaps even making it a little less than it could have been). I was the senior researcher, collaborating with graduate students, but I had taken a "last author" sort of role.[5] I made the mistake of leaving all of these power dynamics implicit and, even worse, trying to treat the whole arrangement like an ungraded democracy. Decisions about scheduling, where and how to edit text, and authorship became territorial squabbles, which I made worse by trying not to make an "executive decision." I still feel some remorse about the anxiety and damaged relationships created by my naïveté and unwillingness to be explicit about power.

This is a small example, but every research project is patterned by countless such localized negotiations of power, resources, time, and other elements of organization. In research, the ways we arbitrate such negotiations and the ways we structure our priorities reflect and embody specific moral commitments (to care, caution, transparency, fairness, etc.) and so are partly determinative of the degree to which the work that flows from them can be called good science.

---

[5] The meaning of author order varies across disciplines, but, in our case, first author was the most prestigious, and last the least; first, the most work or influence, last the least.

Participation

The research consideration probably most often described in moral terms is participation. This makes sense, as the greatest harms in research, both potential and actual, reside in the ways that subjects or participants are (or have been) treated. Those who are subjected to research occupy vulnerable positions, usually without full knowledge or control of research events or outcomes and often without full consent; and those who conduct research benefit from that vulnerability. Abuse is hardly surprising under such conditions and historically (as we have already seen) all too common. It is thus not without reason that most of what we call "research ethics" concerns this relationship. Indeed, most studies will probably have more participants than people who read the report, so how we treat those participants, and our relationships with them, may very well be the most significant legacy of our work. If those relationships are dehumanizing, juvenilizing, trivializing, alienating, objectifying, or oppressive, then we will have spent a great deal of time and effort creating unpleasant, possibly damaging, relationships with the largest group of people who will ever have anything to do with our study.

Obviously, the moral texture of these relationships is incredibly complex, but some of the major considerations can be classed under the notions of choice, voice, and safety. By choice I mean the degree to which the design and execution of research permits self-determination to those who participate. We usually discuss the dilemma of choice in terms of legal consent and, while this is no doubt a fundamental moral consideration in research, genuine choice also requires genuine information and genuine alternatives. Participants can only really choose to participate if they have the opportunity for "ongoing consent" (O'Reilly, Parker, and Hutchby, 2011, p. 181); that is, they must be able to continually evaluate the risks and costs of research and renegotiate consent based on their evolving understanding. This negotiation requires honest and timely information and, even more, a researcher actively seeking consent by trying to understand the vulnerabilities, needs, and changing emotional and mental states of participants.

I recall, for example, a study where the importance of this type of consent became clear. During research trials, an assistant reported an unfinished trial and so I reviewed the video; what I saw was a participant growing increasingly agitated, and eventually distraught, before asking to leave the study. I didn't anticipate this sort of reaction (to what I thought was a pretty mild procedure), and so hadn't tried (and hadn't taught research assistants to try) to check in with participants, provide extra clarifications, or anticipate or watch for signs of distress. It was clear that we hadn't correctly anticipated what the participants' reactions would be and that we didn't provide sufficient monitoring. In effect, this participant hadn't truly consented to the events, because these only became clear in process, and our consent processes were not sufficiently ongoing to take effect in a timely way.

Choice also requires genuine alternatives – that is, those who participate in research cannot really be considered consenting when they have no viable alternatives to their participation. There are many famous examples of this sort of coercion, and these are often discussed in research ethics trainings, texts, or courses. Some common examples include research with institutionalized populations (e.g., US military research on the effects of LSD), with so-called "vulnerable populations" (e.g., mid-century radiation studies with disabled children and poor pregnant mothers), or with those under incarceration or compulsion (e.g., the Minnesota Starvation Study), but there are less dramatic examples of coercion in everyday research. For example, a great deal of research happens through "subject pools" where undergraduates are either required to volunteer for research (with some onerous alternative, like doing extra coursework) or offered extra-credit under competitive grading conditions that make non-participation difficult. There are also all kinds of subtle (and sometimes quite overt) pressures to participate when potential subjects receive treatment at clinics, services at state institutions, resources through social programs, and so on. All of these pressures, unattended, can easily erode the possibility of genuine alternatives.

Like choice, voice is also a primary moral consideration in research participation. By voice, I mean the possibility of genuine participation, respect, and redress. Debates over participant terminology are a good example of how challenging it can be to allow participants a genuine voice in research. In the late 1990s there was a debate between members of the American Psychological Association (APA) and members of the American Psychological Society (APS) about whether "participant" or "subject" was the appropriate term (see Bibace, Clegg, and Valsiner, 2009). The APA favored the former because of its agentic implications, while APS favored the latter because it more accurately depicted the research relationship. Really, it is hard to argue with either position – certainly, most research involves very little "participation" on the part of subjects, a point that Henry Roediger (2004) (then president of APS) made dramatically clear when he referred to college students as the "drosophila" of memory research. Yet, it is hard to find fault with the moral impulse to treat participants as agents, worthy of respect and genuine participation in research; even if "participant" doesn't accurately reflect much of what happens in research, it seems like a worthy aspirational term.

This debate highlights how difficult it can be to show real respect and permit genuine participation in the traditional research environment. We can think of respect as something like basic civility and most psychological research won't encroach too much on that sort of respect. But respect is more than politeness – it is also an acknowledgement of the value of persons and of their unique beliefs, capabilities, and contributions. There are certainly some approaches to research, like participatory and community-based methods, that treat participants as important contributors, even expert collaborators, but this is not the usual research situation. In the very limited researcher–subject interactions of most research, there is rarely, if ever, any engagement with, let alone valuing of or learning from, the subject as a whole and unique person, capable of valuable insight (or resistance). Most researchers will want subjects who elicit very specific behaviors under very constrained conditions while their unique values or contributions will be treated as essentially noise or error.

From a practical (instrumental) point of view, this makes sense; if I'm trying to figure out how priming affects short-term memory, then I'm probably not interested in what each subject thinks or feels about memory or about my research design; I just want clean, unbiased memory reporting. But, even if we take this instrumental attitude to be epistemically justifiable,[6] there is no escaping the fact that it is a morally problematic stance to take toward another person. If, in our everyday lives, someone treated us this way – asked us not to show our uniqueness, not to be our spontaneous selves as complete beings; asked us not to share our thoughts or contributions, but simply to act as a resource, poorly compensated – we would hardly consider that a

---

[6] A chancy assumption, as we have already seen.

respectful relationship.[7] Genuine respect for participants is thus a very difficult standard to meet in most research situations, but we seem to mostly ignore this dilemma, perhaps justifying it as minor or "collateral" damage, incident to the instrumental aims of research.

Of course, if the researcher is always the final word on what harms or negative effects can be considered "acceptable losses" then abuse becomes nearly inevitable. If a researcher can decide that what he will learn from irradiating disabled children is worth the risk – and he doesn't have to explain himself to the children or their parents – then (as history shows) his self-serving risk–benefit calculation will prevail. When participants have no genuine redress – when they don't know or fully understand all that will be done to them and are neither party to risk–benefit calculations nor provided fully informed opportunities to question those calculations nor to seek compensation or censure because of their consequences – then researchers and the institutions they serve simply will not adequately attend to participant needs and vulnerabilities. When participants have no real voice, no real power to challenge (or even participate in) the inevitably egocentric moral calculations of researchers, then even the best-intentioned researchers will not fully appreciate how their work may be harming others, and they will not, despite those good intentions, avoid the historical abuses of research.

And, ultimately, abuse is what research ethics are primarily designed to limit. In most discussions of research ethics, we talk of preventing abuse in terms of non-maleficence (do no harm), an important concept but an unwieldy word, so here I'm using the term "safety." By safety, I mean the moral obligation to protect participants from exploitation, intimidation, or harm. When individuals participate in research, they should have the expectation that their safety won't be compromised; they should know that they won't be hurt, bullied, or taken advantage of. Obviously, when participants have genuine choice and voice, then abuse is much less likely; when they can advocate for themselves, and when we as researchers actively support that advocacy, then participants can serve science by tempering our hubris, egocentricity, and general moral blindness.

---

[7] I am well aware that this describes many folks' working environments; a fact that only supports my contention that this is not a respectful way to treat others.

As always, these various personal and relational dilemmas are complicated by institutional constraints, particularly as attention to "research ethics" is mostly filtered through questions of institutional liability. Discussions of research ethics are almost never about personal moral duties to particular participants, nor about specific participant needs or vulnerabilities, nor even about researcher values. Instead, we think about how to get through a subjects review; and this means that we think about the things most relevant to preventing expensive lawsuits: acquiring written (or at least formal) consent, protecting participant identity, avoiding demonstrable harm, and so on. This institutional aspect of research ethics is not a problem by itself – quite the contrary, it is an indispensable and incredibly important advance in the protection of participants – but it can become a grave liability if it exhausts our moral thinking and actions relative to our participants.

This is, in fact, one of the main points of this entire book: when we sequester moral questions to the very limited domain of institutional review (and liability), we become blind to the vast moral scope of our research activities; we can easily fall into the error of assuming that a successful subjects review accounts for our moral obligations, and this false security can make research abuses more likely. I don't know that any particular changes to institutional review are implied by these arguments; rather, they suggest that the whole research process, from nascent ideas all the way to real-world applications, should be reframed, both conceptually and in terms of actual practices and institutional forms, as a moral endeavor.

Some Questions

What I have tried to describe in this chapter are some of the circuits of mutual patterning that weave together research practices and their moral, social, and political contexts. I have tried to show that, down to its most procedural roots, research is a moral endeavor; that design is not just a matter of fitting sanctioned procedures to their appropriate epistemic ends, but a plotting of the kind of world we want to make through our practices and commitments. When we can see more clearly this moral shape to research (and the way that research is a moral shaping), then we can see more clearly our duties as researchers. We can ask new kinds of questions (as we did in the last chapter) that can help us account for the true scope of our activities.

When we can see that funding is not just a matter of acquiring sufficient resources to conduct research, but that it is an inevitable struggle between epistemic and moral values and the limitations and affordances imposed by resource conditions, then we might ask new kinds of questions about how we fund research. We will ask the usual questions: *How can I get lab space (or institutional access, or bandwidth)? How can I recruit labor (and compensate people for it)? Where will I get the equipment I need? How can I get institutional and administrative support? How can I cover production and publication costs? How much time is this all going to take (and where do I come up with it)? How will I pay (or get people to volunteer) for all of this? How can I get external funding?*

But we might also ask questions like: *What are the costs (financial, human, emotional, etc.) of my research and who is bearing them? What conditions do I have to accept to get access to resources? What compromises will I have to make to meet those conditions? How do those compromises support or undermine my epistemic and moral commitments (and those of my communities)? What institutional or structural requirements constrain my design choices? How do these support or interfere with my commitments (and those of my communities)? Whose values or agendas am I accepting or promoting when I accept certain resources? Whose needs and vulnerabilities am I ignoring when I accept certain constraints? Where and how do I cooperate with or resist these institutional and resource requirements? What are alternative sources of (or models for) funding or resources? What can be done without access to extensive financial or institutional resources?*

When we understand that research space is not just a location, but a set of dwelling practices that express our commitments (to hospitality or hostility; to conservation or consumption) and that shape our communities and environments, then we might ask different kinds of questions about the research homes we build. We will ask the usual questions: *What space (physical, digital, temporal, etc.) is available? How much space is available? When is space available and for how long? What kind of space is available? How can that space be used or configured? What is the condition of that space (lighting, existing furniture, noise/traffic, general repair, etc.)? Where is the space located and how easily can it be accessed? How can I prepare and manage the space to be as free as possible from distractions, equipment malfunctions, research artifacts, and so on?*

But we might also ask questions like: *What forms of dwelling does my research involve? Do these reflect my values (and those of my communities) about how we should live in the world? Are these practices welcoming? Are they hostile? Do these practices cultivate good will (among participants, administrative staff, assistants)? Do they build community? Are they exploitative, arrogant, dismissive, ungrateful, graceless, demanding, or entitled? How do others feel and act when they dwell in the spaces I create? How do my practices of dwelling exploit or conserve physical, natural, and human resources? Do these practices ensure healthy environments? Do they permit long-term dwelling in (and use of) those environments? Do they support the well-being of those who participate in my research? Do they help my community to sustain active, healthy research programs (to flourish and endure)? Do the institutions and communities where I do my research have traditions of responsible dwelling (and use of space)? How do these traditions constrain my dwelling practices? Should (and can) they be challenged?*

When we can see that equipment is not just a set of neutral tools, but a way of extending and transforming our individual and collective embodiment, with sometimes profound consequences for those who participate in (or are subjected to) them, then we might ask different kinds of questions about how we choose to remake ourselves. We will ask the usual questions: *What equipment do I need? What is the best kind of equipment (for my design, my questions, my space, my participants)? What equipment is available? How can I get access to or fund the purchase of adequate equipment? What is the condition of the equipment? How well does it work and how reliable/durable is it? How can I adapt, repair, and maintain the equipment? How does the equipment work? Who knows how to use it? How can I learn how to use it? How well does it work when I test it?*

But we might also ask questions like: *How does the equipment I use (furniture, tools, and space, instruments for recording and analyzing data, measures, devices or structures to manipulate conditions, etc.) shape those who interact with it? How do their actions, experiences, attitudes, and bodies change when they use or are subjected to the use of that equipment? Do they understand and accept those changes? Do those changes reflect their values? Do they reflect my values (and those of my communities)? How does the equipment I use frame persons, relationships, and groups? Is that framing consistent with how*

I understand persons, relationships, and groups? How has the equipment I use already shaped persons, institutions, societies, and cultures? Is that history consistent with what I (and my communities) value? Does the equipment I use have a history of harm or exploitation? Does the nature of that equipment encourage deception, domination, hurt, or exploitation? How is my equipment use constrained by practical, institutional, and disciplinary requirements? Do these constraints encourage responsible equipment use and, if not, how can they be challenged?

When we understand that organizing research is not just about getting things done in the right order and on time, but is a kind of moral ordering (of priorities and persons), a micro-politics of local power, and an expression of our relational commitments, then we might ask different questions about how we order lives. We will ask the usual questions: *What are the basic tasks that need to be completed in my project (and in what order)? How long will these take? What resources do I need to accomplish them? What (and how long) will it take to get those resources? What deadlines (and other bottlenecks) do I have to address? What problems can I anticipate? How can I prepare for them? How can I be efficient in my use of time and resources? Whose help will I need? What (and how long) will it take to get that help? What are the most effective ways to collaborate with others? How can I best handle problems or disagreements? Who will be responsible for each task? How will work be monitored and documented (and by whom)? Who will make final decisions about each of these questions (who will be in charge)?*

But we might also ask questions like: *What are my most important responsibilities in conducting research? Does the order and timing of my planning reflect those responsibilities? What commitments determine my planning priorities? Do these reflect my values (and those of my communities)? How do I dispose of persons (and places) and their time in my planning? What are their needs, capacities, and values? Are the scale and pace of my planning sustainable and respectful of the needs, capacities, and values of others? How do my commitments to institution and discipline constrain my planning? Can (and should) those constraints be resisted? What are my responsibilities to my collaborators? How do I treat them and how should I? Do I show them respect and collegiality? Do I act in good faith? What care do they need? What care can (and should) I give? Can they come to me for help? Am I worthy of their trust? Do I make their work easier (and what do I do that makes it harder)? Do I make their work better (and what do I do that makes it worse)? Do I acknowledge power differentials in my research collaborations or communities? Are these differences in power just? Do they reinforce existing social inequalities (long-standing inequalities based on race, gender, nationality, sexuality, etc.)? Could (and should) they be made more equal? Do I use my power or influence unjustly? How can I fairly arbitrate disagreements? How can I respectfully and effectively respond to complaints, concerns, requests, or objections? Do my collaborators (and subordinates) feel like I have treated them fairly? Do they feel like I have used my influence responsibly? Do I encourage open communication, honesty, and transparency?*

When we can see the participation of others in our research not only instrumentally, nor even solely in terms of institutional ethics, but as a moral call to protect and cultivate the choice, voice, and safety of all who entrust their care to us, then we might ask different questions about research participation. We will ask the usual questions: *How many (and what kinds of) participants will I need for my research? Where (and how) can I recruit them? What resources (including time) do I need to do the recruiting? What permissions do I need to do the recruiting? How do I schedule participants? How can I prepare for scheduling problems? How do I track participation? What help do I need to manage participation? How do I get approval from a subjects review board? How do I obtain participant consent (and possibly consent from parents and others with legal authority)? How do I ensure that participants are adequately informed about the potential risks of participation? How do I ensure that all participants have genuine alternatives to participation in my research and that they are not coerced in any way (and that they know they can refuse to participate at any time without consequence)? How do I ensure that participants are compensated in ways commensurate with the costs or risks they incur? How do I protect the confidentiality (or anonymity) of participants? How do I minimize participant risk or harm (and ensure that these are outweighed by the benefits of the research)? How do I provide protections from harm and redress should it occur? How do I ensure that those who bear the risks of research are those who benefit from it? How do I ensure that my research does not exploit vulnerable populations? How do I ensure that there is no discrimination in the distribution of benefits from my research?*

But we might also ask questions like: *What are my duties to research participants (particularly those not already considered in a standard subjects review)? Does my research dehumanize, trivialize, alienate, objectify, or oppress participants in any way? Do I ensure that participants fully understand the nature and consequences of their participation in my research? Do I ensure that participants can (and do) give full and ongoing consent to all aspects of their participation in my research? What can I do to assess and address the changing vulnerabilities and needs of participants? How can I ensure that participants are treated with respect (and civility)? How do I acknowledge (and ensure that others acknowledge) and respect participants' unique values, beliefs, capabilities, and contributions? How can I ensure that participants have genuine opportunities to question, raise objections, or seek redress? Do I (and how do I) discourage participant autonomy or resistance? How can I include participants in deliberations over risks, costs, and benefits? How can I support participant self-advocacy? Can (and should) I give participants more influence over how the research is conducted? How can I ensure that all participants feel safe (i.e., feel that they will not be exploited, deceived, or hurt)? How can I ensure that all participants are safe?*

While these questions are not (nor were they intended to be) a neutral accounting of the responsibilities we face in designing and conducting research, they are a good faith and, I hope, sufficiently well-wrought example of what it might look like to turn our attention to moral concerns in the design and conduct of research. They are examples of the sorts of questions we might ask together as we try to justify our work as psychological researchers. And, though these questions are neither exhaustive nor definitive, they reveal the shape of our dilemma. They show us that to do research is to meddle in the bodies, lives, and futures of persons, places, and communities and that to treat this as a purely technical undertaking is, to put it baldly, an affront. They show us the wider scope of our responsibilities and invite us to take them up.

10 | *The Interpretation and Reporting of Research*

Data don't interpret themselves (see Part II), so to learn anything from research, we must develop an epistemic frame, constitute evidence within it, and then draw conclusions from that evidence. There is some tendency in writing about science or methods to treat this process as mostly algorithmic and data-driven, but of course, all interpretive acts – including measurement and calculation – involve choices about what matters, what is real, and what constitutes warrant. Interpretation is thus never simply a matter of "reading" the data (much less letting the data speak for themselves), but always an expression of both epistemic and moral commitments.[1] This is true both for how a researcher interprets her own evidence, and also for how her work is interpreted, disseminated, and applied by others. Our research takes on a public life when we say what it means and so interpretation is not just an analytic process, but also a rhetorical and political one. We must fashion persuasive texts, convince someone to publish them, engage in public explanations or defenses of our research, and (at least try to) arbitrate how our work is understood and deployed (in both scientific and practical contexts).

Everything we say in this long conversation about our research reveals and enacts our commitments, and the task of this chapter is to show how and where these commitments are moral ones. To do this, I will focus, first, on the process of constituting evidence and interpreting it, and, second, on the process of writing, publishing, and disseminating research reports.

Interpretation and Analysis (Constituting Evidence within an Epistemic Frame)

Analysis is typically treated as a stage in research, usually coming near the end of a project, but this is a purely heuristic convention. Analysis

---

[1] I already discussed the value-laden and fundamentally interpretive nature of science in Parts I and II of this book, so I won't repeat that discussion here.

124

really begins long before any data are collected. In Chapters 8 and 9, I discussed how domain and theory choice constrain the kinds of choices we can make in research, and the same is certainly true of analytic choices. When we contribute to a research tradition, we are committing to speak in languages intelligible to that community, and this includes employing epistemic frames, analytic procedures, and interpretive languages indigenous to the community. In some traditions, you will be expected to produce operationalizations, frequencies, and effect sizes; in others you will be expected to employ signal detection theory or phenomenology, hypothesis tests or confidence intervals, and so on. Undoubtedly, innovation is possible but not too much or too far (without beginning to speak a different language).

The epistemic frames within which we constitute our analyses are thus, at least in part, pre-given, and so we may not always interrogate these closely. Each time we design a study, we probably won't ask ourselves if we're still empiricists or whether we'll be employing falsificationist logic this time around. These are the mostly implicit background assumptions that warrant the procedures we use and the conclusions we draw. But, to continue my refrain, these epistemic frames are not morally neutral and when they remain invisible, we cannot see or attend to their moral affordances. Our research traditions may, sometimes, choose our analytic methods for us, but they, and their moral histories and implications, are still our responsibility.

In some cases, it is obvious where some interpretive decision is value-driven. Philip Kitcher (2003), for example, has argued that decisions about what to study or what questions to ask cannot be reduced to scientific theory or method, but derive from values and commitments outside of science. These are questions about what *matters*, an unavoidably moral consideration. But even seemingly neutral, or at least purely epistemic, decisions can be seen as value-impregnated. Helen Longino (1995), in fact, has argued that no research commitments are purely epistemic and value-independent. For example, empirical adequacy – or "agreement of the observational claims of a theory or model with observational and experimental data" (p. 386) – is generally described as a purely epistemic value. Longino argues, however, that even if predictions and data coincide in some particular case, there is no guarantee that the data used to make the comparison were (or even could be) selected in some value-neutral way. She discusses various examples, including one where failing to attend to female members of a species led to "distorted accounts of the structure of animal societies," another where toxicity studies failed to adequately account for chemical interactions, and one more where "focus on gene action has blinded us to the ways in which genes must be activated by other elements in the cell" (p. 395). In these cases, the models being tested may have been "empirically adequate in relation to data generated in laboratory experiments, but not in relation to potential data excluded by a particular experimental set up" (p. 395); and those exclusions will always reflect commitments beyond empirical adequacy (e.g., gendered biases about what kinds of data matter most). In other words, even a commitment as seemingly straightforward as empirical adequacy will, in its real-world realization, express (and even require) the moral values of researchers.

One of our moral tasks in developing our own epistemic frames, then, is to disclose (to ourselves and others) these values and attend to their consequences. Such values inhere, from the very beginning of any research process, within the different ways we choose to frame the grounds (or warrants) for theories or inferences to be considered true, justified, correct, and so on. Philosophers of science have suggested a broad range of possible warrants for scientific knowledge, including: those theories or inferences that provide intellectual economy (or the capacity to organize information), that aid in problem-solving, that contribute to prediction and control, that aid in reality-testing, that permit generalization, that are rhetorically convincing, that advance understanding, that help to address practical problems, that fairly represent a plurality, that give voice to others, and many others. Needless to say, such different ways of thinking about warrant will entail different practices and reflect different values. An indigenous researcher with strong commitments to fairness, community practices, and listening will approach what counts as good evidence and good argument in a very different way than will a memory researcher with strong commitments to tightly controlled, generalizable causal inferences.

Proponents of these different epistemic framings tend to interpret their differences from each other in moral terms – that is, in terms of good and bad science (or good and bad knowledge) – and they are not wrong. These are, in fact, moral questions – questions about our commitments, our worldviews, about what science is and should be and where its potentials and dangers lie. These epistemic commitments are different ways of constituting what the value(s) of science *should* be.

Such valuing processes also extend beyond our epistemic frames and into the constitution of particular collections of evidence. There is some tendency to think of evidence as, by itself, an independent warrant for claims.[2] As I have already discussed, however, evidence always underdetermines theory; there are always many ways that evidence can be curated and framed. When we marshal evidence, we make choices about where and how to look, what to include and what to ignore, how to document and interpret. And all of these choices are made within irreducibly ambiguous relationships between evidence and argument, and so they necessarily involve "extra-empirical" considerations and influences (expediency, resource constraints, interpersonal factors, local affordances, political considerations, etc.). There is no escaping the conclusion that I, the researcher (the report writer), am *constituting* the evidence (rather than merely presenting or interpreting it). Evidence, in short, is a rhetorical enactment that reflects the unique constraints of the system within which it operates.

Thomas Teo (2010) has written about one particularly consequential way that evidence from psychological research has been constituted in ways that serve a specific political project. In this process, what he calls epistemological violence, researchers interpret inherently ambiguous data sets in ways that derogate particular groups. He points to, among many other examples, the well-known research on racial differences in intelligence. The data presented in such research permits many possible interpretations – for example, that differences in intelligence are related to historical and environmental factors – but race difference researchers (e.g., Henry Garrett; see Winston, 1998) have often chosen to take these data as evidence for genetic differences, and thus for an interpretation of inferiority among a whole class of persons. Researchers drawing such conclusions have generally presented their interpretations as a courageous fidelity to undeniable scientific facts, rather than as a curation and framing of information that could be understood in many other equally plausible ways. But in these cases, as in all cases of research, the evidence doesn't speak for itself; it must be selected, interpreted, and framed, and the choices we make in that

---

[2] E.g., "That's an empirical question" or "The data speak for themselves" or "What do the numbers say?"

process are moral choices reflecting not only what we believe about the moral position of science, but also our larger value commitments (on issues of race and gender, on immigration politics, etc.).

As in the other elements of research that we have discussed, the inescapably political nature of analytic decisions also extends the researcher's responsibility beyond the laboratory and into the places where politics are arbitrated. An interesting case example reflecting the rhetorical and political nature of epistemic commitments can be seen in the way that evidence-based practice (EBP) has been institutionalized in clinical practice. EBP policy has, since its origins, inscribed a conflict over the "best" kinds of evidence, a conflict characterizing negotiations within the APA Task Force on Evidence-Based Practice (see Lovasz and Clegg, 2019, for a more detailed discussion). In that Task Force, some saw evidence as proceeding from a methodological hierarchy of kinds (with RCTs at the top), while others advocated a more pluralistic approach. The official Task Force statement represented a compromise position and reflected the ongoing tensions between these differing approaches to evidence. However, the rhetorical and professional pressures to represent psychology as scientific have since that time resulted in a set of institutional constraints on accreditation, third-party payer reimbursement, publishing rules, and so on that implement EBP in a way that privileges certain kinds of evidence (principally RCTs) over others.

In this case, we can see that what "counts" as evidence is a kind of political negotiation, arbitrated not only in professional journals or task forces, but in corporate board rooms and legislative chambers. The psychologists who debated the nature of evidence in clinical practice did their work not just in labs but on committees, in forums, and in publications. Likewise, proponents of racial differences in intelligence and their opponents have advocated particular evidentiary framings before congress, in op eds, and in the courts (with far-reaching consequences for millions). Seemingly private decisions about what to analyze and how, about what counts as data, evidence, or warrant, are, in fact, political questions decided, not just in individual minds or labs, but in the various public platforms where we exercise our epistemic citizenship.

Reporting

Research, finally, becomes science when it is published, a process we call reporting, but which is much more complicated than simply telling what we did. The process of reporting is brought to fruition (usually over long spans of time) through an incredibly complex array of moral choices set within particular institutional and interpersonal commitments. In Clegg (2019), I discussed these issues in detail, so I will refer to that work as I outline my main points here. In that earlier discussion, I divided questions of publication and dissemination into five categories: (1) collaboration and credit; (2) style and representation; (3) venue, availability, and audience; (4) submission, editorial, and revision; and (5) dissemination and use.

Regarding questions of collaboration and credit, my main points touched on the equitable distribution of labor and a commensurate distribution of credit or compensation. In my experience, the negotiation of labor and its rewards tends to be relatively explicit and equitable among co-authors of comparable rank. As we saw in our discussion of lab ethnographies (e.g., Knorr-Cetina, 1981; Latour and Woolgar, 1986; Peterson, 2015; see Chapter 4), however, this negotiation is less explicit, and often exploitative, in more hierarchical arrangements – for example, vertically stratified labs, with post-docs, graduate students, undergraduate students, and staff occupying lower social positions and receiving comparably lesser compensation for their labor. In such environments, much of the labor behind reporting and publication is simply invisible, as "proofreading, feedback, formatting, research and other forms of help" are "not always credited or compensated" (Clegg, 2019, p. 87). This unequal distribution of labor and credit is often a normalized feature of lab organization (recall, for example, Roy's experiences, as reported by Knorr-Cetina, 1981; see Chapter 4), and so can obscure various forms of inequity. I described some examples of these:

Some years ago, a student tried to help me see [his challenges] ... and it was startling how much was simply invisible from my relatively secure position. I suggested that his work could benefit from a slower pace, and he reminded me that he wasn't paid a living wage and that his family's well-being depended on a short time to degree; I suggested that he teach less and he noted that his family wouldn't have health insurance if he didn't teach. Another student showed me how minority students in a doctoral program were often not chosen as collaborators or were given work less likely to receive professional credit and how any attempts to seek fairness or compensation were construed as anti-social or distasteful. (Clegg, 2019, p. 88)

Given how easily inequities can be hidden in the graded hierarchies of research, I suggested in that earlier work that, within contexts of collaboration, report authoring, and publication, "practices that permit or encourage the voicing of concern or dissent and listening, that provide formal redress, and that explicitly seek to find and ameliorate unfairness or harm are necessary" (p. 89). I also suggested the importance of acting to transform disciplinary and institutional structures that foment inequities in the distribution of collaboration and credit by, for example, advocating more equitable compensation for low-wage staff or refusing "to contribute to organizations or journals with punitive or exploitative practices" (p. 89).

Beyond the arbitration of labor and credit, the authoring of reports also involves various kinds of rhetorical decisions about style and representation. Though these rhetorical choices are often constrained by disciplinary conventions and style requirements (calling, again, for various kinds of epistemic citizenship), they are still moral stands about what matters and how best to represent ourselves and others. When we write, we choose who to cite (how much and how often), whose (and what kind of) work to promote or critique, what stories, viewpoints, and ideological commitments to represent. We are also making choices about how to represent ourselves and others who contribute to our research. We may, for example, choose to sanitize the disagreements, uncertainties, and failures inherent in the research process (see Kuhn, 1970; Niaz, 2010); or perhaps de-emphasize the perspectives of those with less influence or favor our own interpretations.

When we write reports, we are also shaping how others understand our work, the research process, and, especially in the case of psychology, how they understand human persons and human interaction. This shaping can be intentional and explicit or, as Michael Billig (2011) has noted, ritualized within disciplinary writing conventions – for example, in the way that psychologists "often reify abstract concepts (e.g., self-concept or attachment), conferring upon them ontological status and agency, while hiding our own agency, history, and relational qualities" (Clegg, 2019, p. 90). Billig (2011) also points to the ways that the writers of research reports use nominal forms or passive voice, in the process obscuring the agency and identity of the actors involved, as well as eliding the dynamic and relational processes characterizing research. As I argued in Clegg (2019), "these are not merely stylistic choices; they are choices to obscure the human, social, and moral qualities of the research process and so project a kind of neutral and mechanical façade over the very human process of doing science" (p. 90).

Another set of moral choices (and institutional systems) that report writers navigate are those related to the venue, availability, and audience for published work. When we choose a publication venue we are supporting and, at least tacitly, endorsing a particular set of publishing practices. To publish in so-called "predatory" journals (i.e., those with pay-to-publish-anything models), in journals with histories of support for problematic ideologies (e.g., *Mankind Quarterly*'s history of support for eugenics), or even with publishers that employ steep paywalls, library pricing, and other forms of profiteering (and the resultant discrimination against nations, institutions, groups, and persons without sufficient access and resources), is to become complicit in those practices.

Choosing where and how to publish is thus a decision, both about whose voices should be heard and about who should have access to (and the benefits of) knowledge. Obviously, the degree to which large corporate publishers dominate research publication limits how much researchers can support the best and most morally defensible publication practices. As individuals, however, we can choose where we will publish as well as "post in institutional repositories or work within legitimate open source publication models" (Clegg, 2019, p. 92). We can also significantly shape publication practices directly, as members of editorial teams or as (perhaps online or "boutique") publishers. I have had the opportunity, for example, to help create open access online publications, in the process creating opportunities for younger and non-traditional scholars (as well as those with fewer institutional resources) to both write and read professional research literature. Certainly, most publication is controlled by corporations and not scholars (a curious state in the internet age, particularly as most authors receive no compensation for their work), but it is still our work and so our responsibility.

Participation in the editorial process is perhaps the most significant way that scholars can shape the moral tenor of the publication process. Peer review, for example, is meant to be one of the chief safeguards of scientific integrity, and "so is already an explicitly moral undertaking" (Clegg, 2019, p. 92). Indeed, "the commitments of all involved to scrupulous honesty and fairness, to rigorous attention to texts, and to good faith, collegial review practices" (p. 92) are required for the integrity of scientific work. By the same token, sloppy, manipulative, or dishonest editorial and review practices can undermine the entirety of that project. How we prosecute the editorial process thus constitutes a set of moral choices about how knowledge should be shaped and disseminated.

Of course, just as most authors are largely uncompensated, so also are most editors and reviewers; thus, the integrity of research in psychology often hangs entirely on the good will of those who will do much more than they are paid for. This (very typically neoliberal) arrangement implies the need for both relational care among colleagues and epistemic activism aimed at publishing reform. Having worked as part of different editorial teams, I know the tremendous amount of work each member of the team does, almost entirely out of a sense of dedication to a press or journal and its mission (and certainly not for the non-pay received). I also know how much support members of an editorial team often need from one another – help, for example, finding a reviewer, providing a review when no one else would, or consulting over a manuscript. The moral dilemmas that arise in editorial and publishing contexts are thus not always about knowledge or science, but often about the relational exigencies of shared labor. Experience in editorial work has also shown me the invisible inequities in the publishing system, driven both by corporate greed and by the perverse incentives of academic publishing (Nosek, Spies, and Motyl, 2012; Clegg, Wiggins, and Ostenson, 2020) (among other influences).

Finally, in Clegg (2019), I pointed out that the life cycle of a research report extends well beyond its publication, and so also do our responsibilities for the ways that work is disseminated and deployed. Obviously, researchers can't always control who will read their work, nor how that work will be used, but there are opportunities to shape the way research is consumed. I've already discussed how choices about rhetorical usage and publication venue help determine who will read a report and how that report will be understood. There are also a number of disciplinary processes through which we can continually participate in a discourse about our work – for example, "we can write commentaries or follow-up articles to clarify our positions and correct what we take to be misinterpretations or misuses of our ideas; we can organize symposia to initiate dialogue; we can communicate with colleagues directly" (p. 94), and so on.

Authors can also anticipate how their work will be metabolized in the media or by policymakers and so influence what claims or actions will be made on the basis of that work. A number of journalists, for example, have asked for my comments on a particular body of work and I have learned that this work is likely to be misrepresented without explicit efforts on my part. Consequently, I developed a process where I only provided written comments, where I required that those comments be quoted only in context, and where I wrote the comments in such a way that the ambiguities and limitations of the research couldn't be easily edited out.

More difficult to control are the political uses to which psychological research may be put. "Certainly, the most well-known historical cases where psychology has informed policy – for example, mass testing associated with immigration (Gelb, 1986), military interrogations (Pope, 2016), etc. – do not inspire confidence in our capacity to ensure the equitable and benevolent application of research" (Clegg, 2019, p. 94). Despite these difficulties, researchers can always participate in the political processes where their research is applied – for example, by writing letters, attending hearings, participating in governance, and other forms of activism – and so bear some responsibility to do so.

Some Questions

I will conclude, as I have done in previous chapters, by reflecting on the kinds of questions that a moral geography of everyday research practices inspires. The usual questions that we ask in the process of interpreting our research might include: *What are my research questions and why are these important? What forms of analysis and types of data can best help me to answer those research questions? What forms of analysis and types of data will members of my research community expect me to use or be most persuaded by? What forms of analysis and types of data will I be comfortable with, understand, and have the resources to deploy? Where will I get the resources, including the necessary training, time, help, and equipment, to do the analysis? What assumptions must I make when I employ particular approaches to data collection and analysis? How will I decide which data matter and which I can ignore? How will I decide what constitutes sufficient warrant for my claims?*

These are important questions; however, when we can see our task as not merely the systematic analysis and interpretation of data, but also as a moral stand on what, and whose, questions matter, on the best (even *right*) kinds of data, warrants, or analytic procedures, and a general political stance on what constitutes science and how that science should be deployed, then we may also ask questions like: *Why should I focus time and attention on my research questions (as opposed to other questions I or others might ask)? Why are these questions important? To whom, or for what purposes, are they important and what interests do they serve? Are there other questions that I haven't considered or that might matter more to those from communities or traditions different form my own? How do the forms of analysis and types of data I use, as well as the conclusions I draw, frame persons, communities, and their values? How have these traditions of analysis and data collection been used in the past? Do they have a history of, or potential for, misuse or abuse? In those traditions, and in my interpretations, are individuals or groups derogated when other interpretations are possible? What are the moral implications of my analytic assumptions? What values underwrite those assumptions? What forms of evidence or warrant have I not considered? What might be revealed or concealed by different forms of evidence or warrant? Who was involved in the collection and interpretation of data and how have they been treated (have they been respected, adequately compensated, and represented?)? Whose perspectives and values are represented in my interpretations? Whose perspectives and values have been marginalized, ignored, or silenced in my interpretations? How do my research communities constrain the acceptable kinds of evidence, warrant, and analysis? How could those constraints be challenged?*

Similarly, in the various phases of research reporting, the usual questions we ask ourselves might include: *Who will write the report? How will labor, responsibility, and credit (among other rewards) for authoring be arbitrated and distributed? What forms of organization, formatting, phrasing, and other writing conventions are best suited to my report? What forms are enforced by disciplinary conventions and editorial policies? Where, when, and in what form should I submit my work for publication? What outlets are likely to publish my work? What outlets and formats would best support my work and career? How should I promote my work? How should I respond to requests for further consultation or comment on my work (e.g., from the press, industry representatives, or policymakers)? How should I respond to critiques of my work? What are my responsibilities in the peer review and editorial process? How can I provide fair and rigorous editorial and review?*

These questions, again, are valuable. However, if we can see research reporting as not simply the systematic description of research activities, but also as a form of collective labor involving relational and institutional negotiations, rhetorical enactments of particular voices and values, and the plotting of science and scientific values in the public consciousness, then we may also ask questions like: *Are the costs and rewards of authorship equitably distributed? Do those who conduct the research, write the reports, or contribute to the research in other ways, receive credit and compensation for their work? Are the perspectives and values of those who contributed to the research fairly represented in the reporting? Were the policies governing work and compensation made explicit to research workers and did they consent to these? Were these policies unfair, discriminatory, or exploitative in any way? How can I act to change any unfair policies involved in the production of my research reports? Did those who contributed to the research report have genuine opportunities to voice their concerns or seek redress? Whose perspectives do I emphasize in the writing of the report? Whose perspectives do I de-emphasize or ignore and why? How does my writing represent myself and others? What do I hide, distort, suppress, or misrepresent in my writing? Does the way that I write obscure human dignity or agency, the moral qualities and complexities of research, or the perspectives of those in marginalized positions? How do disciplinary writing and reporting conventions reflect my values (and those of my communities)? How can I act to resist or transform those conventions? How do the publishing practices of the outlets where I submit my work reflect my values (and those of my communities)? Do these outlets support objectionable ideologies or engage in discriminatory or exploitative practices (including locking research behind egregious paywalls)? Who should have access to my work? Who will be denied access to my work and why? How can I influence publishing practices? How does my participation in editorial activities shape what, and whose, perspectives are heard? How do I treat others in my editorial work? How do I support the review and editorial labor that sustains my research communities? How can I help ensure that this labor is fairly and sustainably compensated? How do editorial and publishing practices shape my research communities and how can I act to change them? Is my work reported or deployed in ways consistent with my values (and those of my communities)? Is my work reported or deployed in ways that harm or misrepresent others? How can I shape how my work is reported or deployed?*

As I have said in the other chapters in this section, the technical questions we usually ask ourselves are essential to the effective conduct of science, but only those sorts of morally weighty questions suggested by a moral geography of everyday research practices can help us to fully *justify* psychological science.

11 | Conclusion

The range of possible moral considerations patterning the everyday work of psychological research is obviously vast and far beyond what I have been able to address in this book. I have tried to point to those considerations most salient and pressing, most susceptible to abuse or injustice, but my goal has not been a full accounting. Rather, I have presented these considerations (and the questions that flow from them) as an example of moral attention to the contexts of research from one particular and limited perspective. My purpose in doing so was not to convince the reader that these particular moral considerations are the only ones that matter. Rather, my purpose was to show that this sort of moral consideration reveals the basic structure and nature of scientific activity in a way that a purely epistemic accounting does not; and, even more, that this sort of moral attention orients researchers to the most important questions, dilemmas, practices, and so on required for the prosecution of genuinely good science.

My hope is that this moral accounting has shown how and why we should consider the fundamentally moral framing of psychological research that I have proposed in this book. In this book, I have worked from (and worked to demonstrate) the assumption that all matters of concern in research are ultimately derivative of commitments to what particular scientists and scientific communities take to be *good* (i.e., proper, just, and right). I have argued that scientism, objectivism, and instrumentalism, traditions historically dominant in (particularly North American) psychology, have obscured that moral foundation, sequestering psychological research from the kinds of moral critique that could genuinely *justify* it. I have reframed the notion of *justification*, not as a matter of constructing evidentiary rationales, but as a matter of attending to and refining the whole moral architecture of a scientific community. My argument has been that such justification requires a kind of moral attention, at the disciplinary level, in the form of an open, critical political structure, and at the level of particular research programs, in the form of a research praxis committed to explicit values, as well as to their elucidation and refinement.

I have claimed this collective moral attention as the primary task of psychological research. This is what we should be good at; what we should help our students to be good at; what we should expect other researchers to be good at. This is what *good science* means.

After an argument of this sort, I think two questions naturally occur (at least, these are the sorts of questions I could see myself asking): (1) How can a science founded on moral commitments, for which there are no objective warrants, lay claim to any sort of firm, valid, defensible knowledge? (2) Assuming, for the sake of argument, that we accept this critique and the consequent moral framing of psychological research, how, exactly, will our everyday practices be different?

I address these questions in various ways throughout the book, so I approach them only in their most global sense here. Regarding the status of scientific claims, there is no question that this critique (along with the many other critiques of science from which it borrows) diminishes the epistemic authority of science. Under this account, science cannot be seen as a fully independent or ultimate arbiter of truth. Science, as Bhatia (2019) says, is provincialized; revealed in its local, contextual, and contingent character as a product of particular human commitments and strivings.

However, an attempt to properly contextualize science should not be mistaken for an attack on science; quite the reverse. The greatest disservice to science is to deploy it as a form of cultural domination, as a fiat guaranteeing some local set of value commitments. Insisting on the absolute epistemic privilege of science is a way of making science serve the ends of those who control it, fashioning it as a tool, or as cultural capital, ready to their (our) projects. By contrast, insisting on a moral critique and a moral ordering is a way of serving *science* (rather than serving whoever happens to control its most influential institutions); of making it better for everyone and not simply more useful to a privileged few.

So, yes, a politically, culturally, historically, and morally situated science cannot be understood as the production of unassailable certainties; science is, rather, commitment, under conditions of irrevocable uncertainty, to the best accounts that we can collectively fashion. Those accounts are no less powerful nor useful because they must be justified in their fully human and hermeneutic character. The incredible predictive power abetted by the practices of structural and mechanical objectivity, for example, is not diminished by a recognition of the moral commitments driving and justifying such practices, nor by the acknowledgement that these practices may not serve all legitimate scientific ends. Uncovering the moral context for scientific theories and practices does nothing to undermine claims about their effectiveness, usefulness, or fitness; it only helps us to articulate for whom and for what purposes these theories and practices can be seen as useful or fit. Such moral attention enriches science, drawing on the resources of diverse (and particularly critical and under-represented) perspectives to limit dogmatism and cultural imperialism in science.

On this reading of science, then, we commit to particular scientific accounts, not because scientific certainty compels it, but because we judge them to represent the *best* (in the fullest sense of that term) instantiations of scientific values, integrity, and craft. I have argued here that this is always how scientists have developed consensus; not through some algorithmic adherence to the demands of empirical test, but through reasoned (though not always reasonable) discussion, principled evaluations of scientific work, rhetorical and political persuasion, and other forms of social negotiation. *Scientists*, and not a self-correcting machinery of discovery, validate science and they do so in a fallible, never certain, but still rigorous, principled, reasoned, and responsible way.

Situating science in this way – as irreducibly human and hermeneutic – removes any recourse to the high moral ground of scientism and objectivism, but, as I have tried to show in this book, that high ground was always illusory and constituted little more than cultural fiat. Thus, retreating behind scientism and objectivism has actually weakened scientific claims by sequestering them from the full range of scrutiny required to justify them. Ignoring the social and moral context of scientific claims, in other words, has made it more difficult to tell good scientific claims from bad ones. When the moral and political context of a particular scientific product is strategically erased from reports, presentations, and other discussions, then it becomes much more difficult to assess whether that product represents the values of a particular scientific community (or whether, for example, it is a thinly veiled defense of white supremacy). Under a social and moral account of science, by contrast, we can better situate and more fully explicate the purposes of science work. Thus, relative to the objectivist account of science, the moral framing I propose here can help us lay a much *better* claim to robust scientific knowledge because that claim will not be sanitized of its fundamentally human and moral context. Instead, that claim will be subject to much fuller scrutiny and will more transparently reflect the collective values of the communities it represents.

Now, to the second of my proposed questions: exactly how does the moral account of science change the everyday practices of psychological research? In one sense, there is probably no definitive set of practices by which we might create a more open disciplinary politics or more committed research praxis. There are many ways to more fully justify our work as researchers, many of which I have pointed to throughout the book, but probably none of which is absolutely essential; except, perhaps, for abandoning the ways of working and thinking characterized by scientism, objectivism, and instrumentalism (which, again, is not the same thing as abandoning science or objectivity), and embracing a moral framing for psychological science.

I cannot, therefore, point to any definitive set of normative practices for *good* psychological research; these will vary between context and research community, and will change over time. What is essential, I have argued, is not any particular set of rules for the conduct of research, but an individual and disciplinary framing of psychological research as an everyday moral practice, accompanied by an insistent collective moral attention to that practice (including attendant disciplinary forms and norms conducive to scientific justification). Finding what this looks like in specific research communities is very much an evolving, local labor. Indeed, some readers of this book have likely been working at this labor for years – striving to bring about a more just and moral psychology in their own communities – and so need little instruction in the particulars.

These caveats notwithstanding, for anyone wondering where we might start, I can suggest two very simple ways that anyone could begin to reframe their research practice in the moral terms that I (and many others) have advocated. First, any of us could begin (or continue) to consistently and systematically ask (together with others in our research communities) the sorts of questions I outlined at the end of each chapter in Part III. This would be a genuinely simple thing, and not so hard, but has the potential to radically reframe what we do as researchers. Certainly, the many wise and far-sighted scholars (particularly among feminist thinkers) who have long asked these kinds of questions have radically changed how I think about and do research. If the intentional and programmatic discussion of these sorts of questions became common in research methods texts and classes, in labs where research is designed and conducted, in research oversight, report writing, and editorial, then, regardless of the answers we give to them, I believe that we would begin to think very differently about our responsibilities and about what constitutes good science.[1]

A second thing that any of us could do is to engage in (or continue to engage in) epistemic citizenship aimed at institutionalizing moral and political critique at the disciplinary level. Each of us could turn whatever influence we have toward, for example, making more room (as Helen Longino advocates) in major journals for critical analyses of past and current research traditions; toward more resources for training in critical and historical analyses of science, as well as for journalistic and STS studies of psychological science; toward supporting advocacy that demands more access, in the form of jobs, publication, grants, and so on for under-represented and marginalized groups in psychology; toward support for more disciplinary representation of the problems and values of humanity's majority populations (e.g., those outside of WEIRD contexts); toward publishing and grant reform, aimed at reducing corporate and government influence in research; and toward any of the many other strategies that might build into our discipline a resistance to the status quo.

Of course, these are just two, of many, ways to work at justifying psychological research. If it has done nothing else, I hope this book has inspired you to think of some better ones.

---

[1] In the appendices for this book, I outline various ways that we could fold this sort of questioning into our teaching and mentorship.

Appendix A
Instructor's Guide

Though I did not intend this book to be a research methods text, I wrote it so that it could be used as part of methods instruction and mentoring. How the book might be used in this way may not be immediately clear, so I have included in this appendix a detailed set of recommendations. Appendix A provides a short high-level discussion of the pedagogical approach that inspires these recommendations (which you may wish to pass over if you are only interested in the specific recommendations that follow), followed by chapter-specific recommendations for different levels and types of instruction. Appendix B provides an example curriculum (including schedules, readings, and assignments), based on a Master's-level introductory research methods course. Appendix C provides a list of dilemmas common in research, accompanied by a set of questions meant to inspire moral reflection about those dilemmas (a resource that could be useful in mentored research). The recommendations in these appendices are meant to inspire rather than constrain, so please feel free to ignore them if you have better ideas of your own.

Methods Instruction and Mentorship in Psychology: A Brief Essay

The approach to methods instruction and mentorship that I describe here reflects the approach to science described in this book: I foreground moral considerations and everyday lived practices. By contrast, formal methods instruction in psychology (at least in North America, the pedagogical context with which I am most familiar) tends to be more technically oriented – that is, methods texts and curricula focus primarily on the mechanics of research design and of data collection and analysis (see Clegg, 2016 for an analysis of methods texts in psychology). As a result, readings and concepts from *Good*

Science will likely not fit seamlessly within the typical formal methods curriculum in psychology, particularly at the undergraduate level.

Of course, for those who will actually go on to conduct professional research, most methods instruction happens not in classrooms, but via apprenticeships with practicing researchers (e.g., in research teams or labs) and through Master's theses, dissertations, and other forms of mentored research. The formal methods curriculum can only be a broad introduction to common concepts and forms of practice, while the myriad complexities of research as actually practiced must be absorbed through mentored practice within a particular research community.

Really, no other approach is actually possible, given the incredible complexity of any given scientific subculture. So much of what it means to do research well and responsibly is bound up in a vast, often tacit, domain of community-specific histories, languages, norms, conventions, institutional forms, and professional relationships. There is no way to convey that store of communal wisdom and tradition in a methods text or class; indeed, even if it were possible to articulate the unwritten rules of a research community, this would be of limited general utility, as those rules will vary quite substantially between different communities of inquiry. The norms, shared values, epistemic standards, vocabularies, and so on that we might encounter, for example, in community-based program evaluation research, will be substantially different from those we might find in lab-based memory research. No doubt, many concepts and practices will be shared between such contexts, but being well qualified in one of these research communities simply will not make one well qualified in another; not without extensive socialization to a new set of norms, vocabularies, accepted practices, and so on.

Not just in psychology, but across all sciences, these sorts of distinct epistemic regionalities are the rule rather than the exception. All research is one turn in an ongoing conversation, and this conversation constitutes a community of inquiry. To take part in that conversation and community, researchers must learn to speak that community's language and to observe its forms and norms. Learning to do research has thus always been less a matter of mastering an ahistorical "method," and more a matter of acculturating to a set of epistemic values, institutionalized forms, and traditions of practice specific to a particular research community.

The challenge of teaching methods across such epistemic regionalities is basically a transcultural one; a matter of helping students
develop frameworks and tools for navigating within and between
distinct epistemic cultures. Formal methods instruction in psychology,
however, has tended to either ignore these epistemic regionalities or to
engage with them in superficial or distorted ways and so (in some
ways) has made moving within and between them much more difficult
for novice researchers. Some of the most common strategies for handling these epistemic regionalities in methods instruction include: (1)
cultural assimilation, where all research communities are judged by
standards indigenous to one epistemic culture; (2) cultural appropriation, where practices indigenous to some epistemic culture are
described independent of their historical and conceptual framing; and
(3) cultural isolation, where one particular epistemic tradition is presented and others are ignored or dismissed.

Cultural Assimilation

In the first of these, cultural assimilation, a training program, mentor,
or textbook author presents a unified view of science and/or psychology, an account either stripped of the history of conflict underlying
ideas about what science is and how it works, or characterized as
resolved in favor of one particular view of science. An assimilationist
approach to methods instruction provides universal standards defining
proper science – for example, internal and external validity, or
transparency and reflexivity – and judges all research in terms of those
concepts, including research from traditions whose adherents explicitly
reject those standards. This strategy seems to be the most common.
Certainly, methods texts in psychology tend to present such a unified
view (Clegg, 2016).

In addition to being rather colonial and reductive, an obvious limitation of this assimilationist approach is that it fundamentally misrepresents what students will find when they begin to work in real
research contexts. Young researchers educated in this way may come
to their first research experiences with clean and simplistic assumptions
about science, yet quickly find themselves having to write research
reports and defend their work with considerably more sophistication.

The assimilationist approach to methods instruction leaves new researchers simply unprepared to defend their work adequately. Even more, because this approach will inevitably emphasize some (or even one) traditions of research and marginalize others, it leaves students unfamiliar with, and unprepared to discuss or make use of, a whole array of epistemological tools, forms of design, and methods for data collection and analysis common in some traditions of psychological research.

Cultural Appropriation

The second of these strategies, cultural appropriation, seems to be growing in popularity, particularly in the context of mixed methods instruction. This strategy involves mining different approaches to research for their "techniques" while ignoring or minimizing the theoretical assumptions, value commitments, and histories of conflict underlying those practices. This is basically an eclectic approach, treating research methods like a "toolbox" made up of interchangeable techniques, useful for different purposes, and useable without the need for socialization into the communities of practice from which they are derived (see Wiggins, 2011, for a discussion of the limits of eclecticism in mixed-methods research).

In one sense, the cultural appropriation strategy is a very sensible one; it allows the new researcher to focus on practical questions like design, data collection, and data analysis and remain unmired in the sometimes paralyzing history of methodological conflict. That sense of freedom, however, is misleading, because the realities of academic publishing and presentation will place the novice researcher square in the middle of those conflicts. Editors and reviewers will require explanations for methodological choices; conference attendees will challenge epistemological assumptions; and a theoretically shallow eclectic approach will leave the new researcher unarmed for that conflict. And those reviewers and conference attendees will be right to challenge that eclecticism; all research practices have histories, and to deploy those practices without any sense of that history, without any sense of the commitments it reveals or of the alternative and contested assumptions it rejects, is (as I have argued throughout this book) morally and epistemically dangerous.

Cultural Isolation

The last strategy, cultural isolation, is, I think, becoming increasingly rare. In this strategy, a particular curriculum or text essentially discusses only one view of science and makes no mention of any others. In this approach, students will be taught, for example, Null Hypothesis Significance Testing or Ethnography, and nothing else. Some older methods texts (see Clegg, 2016) take this approach, but every recent (i.e., within the last ten years) text and curriculum that I have seen at least acknowledges an array of methodological approaches and epistemological assumptions. The limitations of cultural isolation are, it seems to me, obvious, so I won't belabor them here – adequately preparing our students for research in psychology requires instruction in at least a partial sampling of the many methodological and epistemological approaches they will encounter (and perhaps require for their research).

Each of these approaches to representing psychological research (assimilation, appropriation, and isolation) shares a limitation – namely, they each, in different ways, ignore or oversimplify the moral and epistemic geography of psychological research and so leave students unprepared for what they will encounter as professional researchers. To adequately navigate the cultural plurality that we call psychological science, new researchers need, not a synoptic account of science, nor an atheoretical survey of techniques, but help developing a kind of epistemic transcultural competence. They need to be able to recognize the regionality of epistemic cultures and to develop tools for navigating responsibly within and between those regionalities.

I would argue (based on my own experiences mentoring novice researchers and on the kinds of arguments made in this book) that this sort of transcultural competence requires at least three things: (1) the ability to provincialize epistemic cultures (as opposed to universalizing them as ahistorical criteria); (2) opportunities to acculturate to different epistemic regionalities; and (3) a critical-moral framework for comparing and evaluating different epistemic cultures and their products.

Learning to Provincialize Epistemic Cultures

Before students can even begin to navigate the multicultural landscape of psychological inquiry, they have to be able to see it. Most novice researchers (at least, nearly all that I have taught) will begin with a generalized and universalized notion of science, scientific method, and psychology. They will not see psychological research as a history of complex and competing values, traditions, norms, and so on, but as a single, unified tradition. A first responsibility in research mentorship is thus to help students learn how to provincialize epistemic cultures in psychology; to help them see those different cultures and understand that they have unique (and sometimes competing) values, assumptions, traditions, and forms of practice.

There are many ways to do this, but, in my experience, the most powerful is to learn a little history. For example, even a short and very simplified account of the "method wars" (i.e., the long history of debate between broadly qualitative and broadly quantitative methods) can sensitize students to different epistemic regionalities. Indeed, a discussion of any of the many episodes of methodological debate in the history of psychology can help to provincialize methods (as I discuss in the recommendations below, some elements of this book can be used for that purpose; Pryiomka and Clegg, 2020 can also be helpful here). Every aspect of psychological method inscribes a history of debate that, even in very schematic form, can help new researchers understand the social geography of research. In testing and validity research instruction, for example, discussions of the role of values in testing (e.g., as reflected in Samuel Messick's work) or of the ways that tests can be deployed politically (e.g., as reflected in the work of George I. Sanchez) can help students better understand the purposes and consequences of psychological testing. Or, to draw on a more recent example, discussions of questionable research practices or of the replication crisis can help to reveal some of the complexities of research politics.

It can also be very helpful to look at perspectives on, and approaches to, psychological research in different geographic and ethnic regions. For example, an overview of research inspired by the Liberation tradition, coming primarily from Latin America (but also traveling to many other locales), can be a very effective way to highlight ethnocentrism in North American (and Western European) approaches to psychological research and to point to the ways that different commitments and traditions of knowing can radically reframe the priorities and practices of research. In general, discussions of research from a multicultural perspective – for example, discussions of coloniality, ethnocentric

sampling, or indigenous methods – can do much to reveal the culturally specific frameworks shaping research.

Learning to Acculturate to Epistemic Regionalities

As new researchers are exposed to this historical and social context,
they acquire the habit of, and tools for, uncovering such context in
their work and in the work of other researchers. In the process, they
can start to map the epistemic geographies that they will move within
and between. Moving within those geographies, however, requires not
just seeing them, but also becoming acculturated to them – that is,
absorbing the vocabularies and norms, decoding the institutional
forms and practices, and engaging with the values of a research tradition (among many other forms of cultural learning).

This sort of acculturation can take place in classrooms, but probably
most often happens in mentored research. Wherever it takes place, it is
really only effective when new researchers are being exposed to actual
examples of the epistemic regionality to which they are attempting to
adapt. Generalized or abstracted accounts, based on a standard lexical
or procedural boilerplate (as in texts or curricula deploying the strategies of cultural assimilation or appropriation), often just create a layer
of oversimplified discourse that has to be unlearned (or, at least,
relearned in a more sophisticated form) in real research practice. By
contrast, when research practices are presented, and experienced, in
their real-world contexts, students can begin to acculturate to their
many nuances. When students read actual examples of research
reports, when they are exposed to debates and historical changes
within research traditions, when they are encouraged to model report
writing or design from published studies, when they work in mentored
research, they experience research as it really is.

Of course, if students are only given opportunities to begin acculturating to a narrow set of epistemic regionalities (perhaps even to a single
one), then they will still be very underprepared for professional
research. A methods curriculum embracing the full diversity of psychological research is, no doubt, impossible, but methods instructors need
at least a schematic understanding of that overall epistemic geography,
such that they can help novice researchers anticipate and navigate it.
Even more than this, those of us who mentor new researchers need
experience with multiple epistemic regionalities and some sense of how

these function differently if we are going to model epistemic transcultural competence for our students.[1]

Learning to Evaluate Epistemic Cultures

A final requirement for this sort of transcultural competence, and from my perspective (and from the perspective outlined in this book) the most important, is a critical-moral framework for comparing and evaluating different products and practices from different epistemic cultures. This sort of framework is important, in part, because navigating different epistemic regionalities is incredibly confusing without some set of standards or other grounds for comparison. If all we do is show new researchers the inconsistencies, disagreements, and ambiguities patterning real-world research, then we will only sow confusion (and perhaps disillusionment). All of us, including our students, need ways to think critically about the differences we find within and across epistemic regionalities and to make responsible, informed evaluations of the practices and products from those regionalities.

Of course, there is no single nor universal critical framework for evaluating psychological research. Research, as I have argued in this book, is justified in terms of the value commitments underlying those communities where the work is conducted, published, and applied. Such commitments are hammered out between community members and across a shared history, and will vary across region and time (and often between members of a research community). Certainly, some of the values justifying research will flow from larger communities – for example, disciplines and subdisciplines; even science or society – and so will be general enough that they can serve as criteria for comparing across epistemic regionalities. For example, commitments to honesty, beneficence, or logical consistency can probably serve to evaluate the products of any research tradition. Nevertheless, every research community will be rooted in a unique set of values, not generalizable to all other communities.

---

[1] Given the increasingly collaborative nature of research in psychology, perhaps the simplest way to expand the range of transcultural exposure for ourselves and for our students is to work in research partnerships and collaboratives that include intersections of different epistemic regionalities; probably many of us already do this and have seen how valuable it can be for new researchers.

This regional epistemic specificity means that there is no general set of norms or commitments that new researchers can simply pick up and deploy. However, as I have claimed throughout this book, though the commitments shaping different epistemic regionalities are different, those commitments all share the same basic moral character. In other words, whatever local standards apply, all work in psychology is justified in terms of value commitments. Thus, though there is no way to predetermine the values for any given community, each individual researcher or community of researchers *can* develop a framework for evaluating research in the same way – that is, through collective moral attention to (and active epistemic citizenship meant to shape) the practices and institutions framing research. What our students need from us, then, is not just to transmit to them a set of canonized norms, but a modeling of the sustained moral attention through which shared values can be arbitrated. Every researcher will decide what commitments she honors and what practices and communities best reflect those; our job as mentors is just to show where those commitments reside in research and how to interrogate them responsibly.

The primary purpose of this book is to help researchers engage in this sort of moral reflection, and so many of the curricular examples and suggestions in these appendices are focused on using the book in this way. I discuss ways of reading the book that could be used to explain the importance of a moral framing for research, describe exercises meant to inspire moral reflection about research, and outline curricula shaped by the kind of research mentorship I describe in this essay. These recommendations are just a sampling of possible strategies, and just one way of approaching curriculum, but they are all reflective of the framework I have outlined here. They are anchored by a view of research instruction and mentorship as a process of encouraging epistemic transcultural competence, via contextualized and historicized accounts of research practice, opportunities to acculturate to a plurality of actual research practices, and the modeling of sustained moral attention as the proper context for evaluating research practices and products within and between epistemic regionalities.

Ways of Using This Text in Teaching and Mentoring

In what follows, I provide some suggestions for using this text as part of research mentoring or formal curriculum. I start with ways that elements of the text could be assigned as targeted readings for specific purposes. I then discuss ways of using the text at different curricular levels, from undergraduate to doctoral instruction.

Targeted Readings

Each of the chapters in this text are sufficiently self-contained that they could be assigned as targeted readings serving various purposes. For very general discussions of the concepts and overall argument in this book, the Introduction is complete enough (including a detailed outline of each chapter) that it could be assigned as written. The Introduction was written to be general and accessible, and so could be assigned to students at any curricular level as a way to expose them to critical and moral accounts of psychological research. The Introduction could also be useful as a companion to other individual chapters from the text, showing how those chapters fit within the larger argument.

Part I of the text provides an overview of critiques commonly found in discussions of science and of psychology. Students and new researchers are likely to encounter these critiques in various contexts (thesis defenses, conference presentations, reviewer comments, etc.), so chapters in this section could be useful for preparing students to understand those critiques. The section as a whole constitutes an integrated critique of epistemological concepts common in psychology and so could also be useful in instructional or mentoring contexts where the goal is to complicate the standard research narratives in psychology or to prepare new researchers to understand alternative conceptions of research (e.g., prior to teaching about non-mainstream forms of inquiry like participatory, indigenous, or qualitative research). Part I is also a fairly accessible introduction to basic philosophy of science questions in psychology and so could be used as a reading introducing science theory (e.g., as an early reading in a graduate methods course).

Chapter 3 (in Part I) discusses instrumentalism in psychology, but also provides an accessible, yet wide-ranging, accounting of exploitation and harm in psychological research. This chapter could thus be useful in a variety of contexts where the goal is to sensitize new researchers to the moral dangers inherent in research. For example, I assign this chapter near the beginning of a Master's-level research methods course as a way of helping students understand why they need to reflect carefully on the consequences of their research designs. This chapter could also be used as part of lectures, discussions, or mentoring addressing research ethics, the history of psychological research, or alternative and critical approaches to inquiry.

In general, Part I focuses mostly on well-established critiques and so, as a targeted reading, is useful primarily as an introduction to key concepts in science theory. Part II, by contrast, includes more advanced and contemporary concepts in science theory and also includes a number of arguments specific to this book. Much of Part II is thus pedagogically useful only in the context of representing the core arguments from *Good Science*. For that purpose, the introduction to Part II is particularly useful, as it provides a fairly accessible introduction to the whole argument. Combining this with Chapter 5 should give readers a clear idea of the alternative conception of scientific justification that I advocate in Part II. Of course, the whole of Part II will provide the most detailed introduction to these ideas.

Individual chapters from Part II could also serve various other purposes. Chapter 4 presents a fairly extensive overview of concepts from the historical and social science studies of science, including from such studies in psychology. This chapter could thus be useful as an introduction to science studies as these apply to psychology or as an overview of the everyday practices new researchers could expect to encounter in research environments. Chapter 6 also includes brief introductions to decolonizing and feminist critiques of, and approaches to, psychological research, so this chapter (or elements of it) could be useful for introducing students or new researchers to those traditions. Chapter 7 also includes simplified overviews of reflexivity and transparency (in the context of moral reflection in research) and so could be similarly useful in discussing those concepts.

Part III of the text is probably the most directly useful for research instruction and mentoring, as the chapters focus entirely on concrete descriptions (including examples) of various aspects of research in psychology; each chapter also includes an extensive list of questions meant to help researchers reflect on their practices. Chapters 8–10 each address different aspects of research and so could be assigned individually or collectively, depending on what an instructor or mentor wishes to cover. These chapters should help students or new researchers better understand the kinds of practices that different stages of research entail. The questions at the end of each of these chapters could also be used in various forms to inspire reflection and discussion about the moral dilemmas and duties involved in research practices. I have used these questions, for example, in class discussions, lab meetings, discussion boards, and writing assignments (a modified and expanded version of these questions can be found in Appendix C).

Much of the content in Chapters 8 and 10 deals with professional aspects of psychological research (theory choice, publication, etc.) and so these chapters may be most useful in teaching or mentoring practicing, graduate-level researchers. Chapter 9, however, focuses on basic research practices that anyone learning to do (or even consume) research should understand. Accordingly, Chapter 9 could be a useful reading for essentially any context involving research instruction or mentoring. For example, I assign this chapter near the beginning of a Master's-level research methods course as a way of sensitizing students, both to the real practices of psychological research, but also to the kinds of moral questions that help to justify that research.

The final chapter (Chapter 11) summarizes the book as a whole and so could be useful in concert with the Introduction and, perhaps, the overviews at the beginning of Parts I, II, and III, as a way of providing a detailed overview of the book. By itself, however, this chapter is probably of limited utility as a reading assignment.

Undergraduate Curriculum

Good Science, as a complete text, would not be suited to most undergraduate research courses. The book is aimed at professional readers who already have some understanding of the basic concepts and practices involved in psychological research. Some individual chapters, however, are fairly accessible and could be used in the targeted ways described above; in particular, Chapters 3 and 9 could be assigned in most undergraduate courses, and Chapter 4 could be useful for advanced undergraduates (see discussion above).

These caveats notwithstanding, there are a few ways that the complete book could be profitably employed in undergraduate research instruction. First, a methods instructor could make use of the concepts from the book, including the questions at the end of Chapters 8–10 and the resources included in this appendix, as they plan courses and curricula. Some ideas for how to do this could be gleaned from the detailed example curriculum (readings, assignments, etc.)

included in Appendix B. And, second, in mentored research with undergraduates (volunteer work in faculty labs, honor's theses, directed readings courses, etc.), the most advanced students should be able to work through the principal elements of this text, with guidance from faculty, graduate students, and other advanced undergraduates. This might work best as part of something like a lab reading group, or perhaps in directed research, reading, or seminar courses.

Introductory Graduate Curriculum

I have used elements of this book as part of an introductory research methods course designed for Master's-level students, and the example curriculum included in Appendix B is based on that course. Students in that class who had taken research courses and participated in mentored research in their undergraduate education were prepared to read and understand *Good Science* without difficulty. For students without such exposure to the concepts and practices of psychological research, however, some of the chapters in this book could be difficult to understand. For this reason, in my course (where not all students have typically had the same level of preparedness) I assign only the most accessible chapters as readings (Chapters 3 and 9). I integrate other elements of the book through exercises, lectures, and assignments (see below) designed for a student of any level of preparedness.

That example curriculum is just one way that *Good Science* could be used, and focuses specifically on an introductory graduate curriculum intended for students of differing levels of preparedness. For students who have received undergraduate methods instruction and who have had some experience working in professional research, any of the chapters in this book should be sufficiently accessible. However, some elements of the book might be difficult to read out of context. For example, for a Master's-level graduate student, Chapters 5–7 would probably be challenging reads if these were not preceded by the first four chapters.

In contrast with undergraduate methods instruction, *Good Science*, in its entirety, could work effectively as part of some graduate methods courses. This book could be profitably assigned as a companion reading in a methods course, or perhaps as part of a research ethics course. Of course, this book does not cover technical elements of research design, data collection, or analysis, and so would not be adequate as the sole textbook for such a course. The targeted readings described above could also be useful individual assignments for courses of this sort. Just as in my recommendations for the undergraduate curriculum, for introductory graduate methods instruction and mentorship, this book could also work as part of training in research labs or in directed research, reading, and seminar courses.

Doctoral-Level Curriculum

At the doctoral level, where most students will be engaging in their own granted and published research, there are no real limitations to how *Good Science* could be used – that is, any of the chapters or sections could be assigned in any combination and I would expect doctoral students to be able to understand and make good use of the material. Therefore, all of the suggested targeted readings listed above could be helpful for graduate students looking for ideas, background, clarity, and so forth on the various topics addressed in the book. That said, I think (perhaps not surprisingly) that the best use that a doctoral-level graduate student could make of this book is to read it, perhaps in a reading group or in a directed readings course.

The way that I most use this text in my own work with doctoral students is not in any particular course but through the process of research mentoring. This mentoring may include encouraging students to read *Good Science*, but happens more often through informal discussion. Especially useful is the process of conducting discussions of research design, data collection and analysis, publishing, and other practical research topics in a way that centers the kind of moral attention advocated in this book. Appendix C includes a set of dilemmas and related questions that could be helpful in this sort of mentoring.

Appendix B
An Example Master's-Level Curriculum

What follows is a detailed fourteen-week curriculum for a Master's-level introductory research methods course integrating readings and concepts from this book. The exercises, readings, and assignments described below are based on a course that I teach, with some modifications. So that the overall curricular structure is clear, I have included references to readings and assignments not directly related to the content in this book, but I have left out detailed descriptions and references for those items. For exercises and assignments that are based on this book, I have included the full descriptions (as well as the references for any associated readings). Some of these descriptions have been modified to make them more general to any research methods course of a similar level.

The outline below includes the following reading assignments from this book:

Week 2: *Good Science*, Chapter 3
Week 3: *Good Science*, Introduction to Part II and Chapter 9

In addition to assigning these chapters from the book, the primary way that the concepts from the text are integrated into the curriculum below is through exercises asking students to reflect on their own research in the context of the moral questions raised here. This is accomplished primarily through exercises integrated with lecture material, weekly individual reflections, and class discussions.[1]

Week 1

Exercise: What Are my Questions? The major assignment in this course is a proposal for a three-study research project. That project will be

---

[1] The curricular structure below reflects the sudden move to online instruction precipitated by the 2020 pandemic, but any of these items can work in other instructional modes.

guided by a single central research question, investigated using three different methods (experimental, quantitative non-experimental, and qualitative). So, your first job in this course is to come up with a research question. To help you get started, complete the following journal prompt:

Think about the following questions and write down your thoughts: *What kinds of research am I interested in? What kinds of research are important to me? What kinds of research am I (or might I be) good at? What kinds of research will be useful to me in my career?*

Choose a general research question to start with – something like, "Is there a relationship between social attention and social anxiety?" – and write it out at the end of this prompt.

Reading: Faculty Profiles
Lecture: Searching the Literature
Tutorial: Index Searching
Exercise: Annotated Bibliography
Reflection: Why Do my Questions Matter?

Each week, you will be asked to write a reflection on the moral context of your research. These entries will ask you to consider the values that guide your research, the histories of, and potentials for, exploitation, injustice, or harm inherent in your research, the needs and vulnerabilities of those who participate in your research, and related questions.

For this week's assignment, reflect on the following questions, then compose an entry that addresses them: *Why should I focus time and attention on my research questions (as opposed to other possible research questions)? Why are these questions important? To whom, or for what purposes, are they important and what interests do they serve? Are there other questions that I haven't considered or that might matter more to those from communities or traditions different from my own?*

Week 2

Lecture: Developing a Research Question
Exercise: What Is my Research Question?
Lecture: Exploitation, Harm, and Injustice in the History of Psychological Research
Reading: *Good Science*, **Chapter 3**
Reflection: What is Good Research?

Each week you will be asked to write a reflection on the moral context of your research. These entries will ask you to consider the values that guide your research, the histories of, and potentials for, exploitation, injustice, or harm inherent in your research, the needs and vulnerabilities of those who participate in your research, and related questions.

In Chapter 3 of *Good Science*, you read about some of the exploitation and harm that are part of psychology's history (and present). In this entry, you will reflect on the moral histories of those traditions drawn upon in your research. You can use the chapter to help you answer the following questions, but you may need to do additional research on the history of those traditions that you are drawing from. Reflect on the following questions, then compose an entry that addresses them: *How have the traditions of research that I am drawing on contributed to justice, human flourishing, or other human goods? How have they contributed to injustice, exploitation, discrimination, harm, or other acts inconsistent with what I (and my communities) value?*

Week 3

Lecture: Writing a Literature Review
Exercise: Writing a Study Overview
Tutorial: APA Style Workshop
Assignment: Literature Review
Lecture: Good Design
Exercise: Good Style

A simple example of the way that moral questions are relevant to every aspect of research design is in the way that we write research reports. Until fairly recently, researchers wrote primarily in passive voice – for example, "Participants were selected based on gender." In this sentence, the writer disguises the identity and agency of the researchers, in the process hiding which particular persons are responsible for which specific actions. The authors of APA style guides have begun discouraging passive voice, suggesting sentences like "We selected participants based on their gender." However, authors use other strategies to hide identity and agency – for example, phrases like "Results suggest ..." hide the fact that a particular author has interpreted a particular set of facts to suggest something (as opposed to the facts just speaking for themselves).

Look through your Literature Review draft and find instances where you have obscured identity (who is speaking or acting) or agency (a particular choice or action), and try rewriting those phrases in a way that shows identity and agency. In the entry below, write one example of a sentence that disguises agency or identity, followed by the rewritten sentence.

Reading: *Good Science*: **Introduction to Part II and Chapter 9**
Reflection: Agency, Identity, and Writing

Each week, you will be asked to write a reflection on the moral context of your research. These entries will ask you to consider the values that guide your research, the histories of, and potentials for, exploitation, injustice, or harm inherent in your research, the needs and vulnerabilities of those who participate in your research, and related questions.

As you work on your Literature Review, reflect on the following questions, then compose an entry that addresses them: *How does my writing represent myself and others? What might I hide, distort, suppress, or misrepresent in my writing? How does the way that I write obscure human dignity or agency, the moral qualities and complexities of research, or the perspectives of those in marginalized positions? How does the way that I write emphasize human dignity or agency, the moral qualities and complexities of research, or the perspectives of those in marginalized positions?*

Week 4

Lecture: Experimental Design Theory
Exercise: Why Experiments?
Reading: Experimental and Quasi-Experimental Designs
Exercise: Your Research Question as an Experiment
Reflection: How do I Protect my Participants?

Each week, you will be asked to write a reflection on the moral context of your research. These entries will ask you to consider the values that guide your research, the histories of, and potentials for, exploitation, injustice, or harm inherent in your research, the needs and vulnerabilities of those who participate in your research, and related questions.

At this point, you should have started to imagine possible experimental studies based on your research question. Take some time to reflect on what it would be like to be a participant in the experimental designs you have imagined. *What will you ask participants to do (or not do)? Where will you ask them to go? What will you tell them and what will you conceal from them? What will you ask of them and what will you give to them?*

When you feel like you have a good sense of what it might be like to be a participant in your experimental study, reflect on the following questions and then compose an entry that addresses them: *How might my research dehumanize, trivialize, alienate, objectify, or oppress participants in any way? How could I ensure that all participants feel safe (i.e., feel that they will not be exploited, deceived, or hurt)? How can I ensure that all participants will be safe?*

Week 5

Lecture: Experimental Designs
Exercise: Experimental Design Review
Reading: Example Experimental Study
Reading: Experimental Design
Lecture: Confounding Variables
Exercise: Anticipating Confounding Variables
Reflection: What Role will Participants have in my Research?

Each week, you will be asked to write a reflection on the moral context of your research. These entries will ask you to consider the values that guide your research, the histories of, and potentials for, exploitation, injustice, or harm inherent in your research, the needs and vulnerabilities of those who participate in your research, and related questions.

As you work on designing Study 1, think about the kinds and degree of influence that participants would have in a study like the one you are designing (influence over how they are treated, over how the experiment will be conducted, over how data will be used, etc.). Now, reflect on the following questions and then compose an entry that addresses them: *How can I ensure that participants in my study will have genuine opportunities to question, raise objections, or seek redress? How can I include participants in deliberations over the risks, costs, and benefits of participating in my study? How can I support participant self-advocacy? Can (and should) I give participants more influence over how my research is conducted?*

Week 6

Reading: Troubling Calls for Evidence

Fine, M. (2012). Troubling Calls for Evidence: A Critical Race, Class and Gender Analysis of Whose Evidence Counts. *Feminism and Psychology*, 22 (*1*), 3–19. doi:10.1177/0959353511435475.

Lecture: Some Moral Questions in Experimental Design

Class Discussion: Some Moral Questions in Experimental Research Design

In this class discussion, I want us to consider the relationship between the choice of an experiment as a research design and questions of justice, fairness, or equality. Here are some questions that you might consider: *How could an experimental design hide injustice? How could it reveal injustice? How could the pursuit of internal validity contribute to inequality? How could it contribute to equality? How much does a researcher need to think about questions of social justice, fairness, or equality in the choice of a research design?*
Your responses do not need to try and provide answers to all of these questions; these are only meant to help you think through the core question (instead, your responses should be your own thoughts on the core question). The core question you should address in your responses is, *When and how can the choice of an experiment as a research design become a question of justice, fairness, or equality?* Your responses can be a stand-alone post of your thoughts on these questions or direct responses to your classmates (or both).

Reading: The Baby Factory

Peterson, D. (2016). The Baby Factory: Difficult Research Objects, Disciplinary Standards, and the Production of Statistical Significance. *Socius*, 2, 2378023115625071.

Lecture: Questionable Research Practices

Exercise: Questionable Research Practices

The Peterson reading describes some Questionable Research Practices (QRPs) that he observed in psychological laboratories. The quotes below are examples of a few of these:
A researcher, talking to the parent of a child research subject: "During the trial, we ask you to close your eyes. That's just for the journals so we can say you weren't directing her attention. But you can peek if you want to. It's not a big deal. But there's not much to see" (Peterson, 2016, p. 4).
A researcher describing how hypotheses were generated: "You want to know how it works? We have a bunch of half-baked ideas. We run a bunch of experiments. Whatever data we get, we pretend that's what we were looking for" (Peterson, 2016, p. 6).

In this journal, reflect on the following questions and compose an entry that addresses them: *What exactly is problematic in these two examples? How could you avoid these and other QRPs in your own research? Why might QRPs be considered a moral or ethical issue in research?*

Reflection: What Kinds of Research Spaces do I Create?

Each week, you will be asked to write a reflection on the moral context of your research. These entries will ask you to consider the values that guide your research, the histories of, and potentials for, exploitation, injustice, or harm inherent in your research, the needs and vulnerabilities of those who participate in your research, and related questions.

As you write Study 1, think about the spaces you would need to create in order to conduct this research (rooms where participants complete the study manipulations, websites where they fill out forms, etc.). Try to imagine those spaces and what it would be like to be in them; imagine what your participants would do there. Now, reflect on the following questions and compose an entry that addresses them: *How are the spaces I create through my research welcoming? Do they cultivate good will, create community, support the well-being of those who participate, and so on? How are they hostile? Are they exploitative, arrogant, dismissive, ungrateful, graceless, demanding, or entitled? How do others feel and act when they dwell in the spaces I create?*

Assignment: Study 1

Week 7

Lecture: Quantitative Non-Experimental Designs
Exercise: My Question as a Quantitative Non-Experimental Design
Reading: Quantitative Non-Experimental Designs
Reflection: What is my Evidence?

Each week, you will be asked to write a reflection on the moral context of your research. These entries will ask you to consider the values that guide your research, the histories of, and potentials for, exploitation, injustice, or harm inherent in your research, the needs and vulnerabilities of those who participate in your research, and related questions.

As you work on designing Study 2, think about the kinds of evidence that you would gather (survey responses, measurements, recordings, etc.). Now, reflect on the following questions and compose an entry that addresses them: *What forms of evidence have I not considered (list as many as you can think of)? For each of these kinds of evidence (including the kind you will gather in Study 2), what aspects of my question, of the phenomenon of interest, or of people's experiences might be concealed, overlooked, or undervalued because I chose this form of evidence?*

Week 8

Lecture: Construct Validity
Exercise: Writing about Construct Validity
Reading: Example Quantitative Non-Experimental Designs
Reflection: How does my Equipment Shape Others?

Each week, you will be asked to write a reflection on the moral context of your research. These entries will ask you to consider the values that guide your research, the histories of, and potentials for, exploitation, injustice, or harm inherent in your research, the needs and vulnerabilities of those who participate in your research, and related questions.

As you design Study 2, think about the kinds of equipment you would need to conduct the study (furniture, tools, instruments for recording and analyzing data, measures, devices, or structures to manipulate conditions, etc.). Now, reflect on the following questions and compose an entry that addresses them: *How will the equipment I use shape or influence those who interact with it? How will their actions, experiences, attitudes, or bodies change when they use or are subjected to the use of that equipment? Will they be able to understand and accept those changes? Does the equipment I will use have a history of harm or exploitation? Does the nature of that equipment encourage deception, domination, hurt, or exploitation?*

Week 9

Readings: Questionable Research Practices
Arnett, J. J. (2009). The Neglected 95%: A Challenge to Psychology's Philosophy of Science. *American Psychologist, 64* (6), 571–574. doi:10.1037/a0016723.
Simmons, J. P., Nelson, L. D., and Simonsohn, U. (2016). False-Positive Psychology: Undisclosed Flexibility in Data Collection and Analysis Allows Presenting Anything as Significant. In A. E. Kazdin and A. E. Kazdin (eds.), *Methodological Issues and Strategies in Clinical Research, 4th ed.* (pp. 547–555). Washington, DC: American Psychological Association. doi:10.1037/14805-033.

Teo, T. (2010). What is Epistemological Violence in the Empirical Social Sciences? *Social and Personality Psychology Compass, 4* (5), 295–303. doi:10.1111/j.1751-9004.2010.00265.x.

Wiggins, B. J., and Chrisopherson, C. D. (2019). The Replication Crisis in Psychology: An Overview for Theoretical and Philosophical Psychology. *Journal of Theoretical and Philosophical Psychology, 39* (4), 202–217.

Exercise: P-hacking Demonstration

The link below represents an actual data set, organized to let you use real data to assess the effects on the US economy of Republican or Democrat office holders. The controls allow you to manipulate various statistical decisions and observe how these alter the data set. Experiment with different options and observe how the results change. You should be able to use the same data set to reflect essentially completely opposed conclusions. The point of this exercise is to show that the kinds of everyday decisions that researchers make in data analysis can have a profound impact on what the data seem to say. Data, in other words, don't ever speak for themselves, but require interpreters; and those interpreters can use the very same data to come to very different conclusions.

https://projects.fivethirtyeight.com/p-hacking/

Lecture: False Positives
Lecture: The Neglected 95%
Exercise: The Cultural Values of my Research

Think about your research project, as you have designed it so far (Literature Review, Study 1, and Study 2). Identify two ways that you will interact with participants (sending a recruitment email, conducting an interview, administering a survey, paying participants, etc.). For each of these two forms of participant interaction:

1) Describe how that interaction reflects your values and culture.
2) Describe how that interaction might conflict with the values or cultures of others.
3) Describe how you could make that interaction more culturally informed and representative.

Lecture: Epistemological Violence
Class Discussion: The Potential for Epistemological Violence in Psychology[2]
In this discussion, I want us to reflect on the potential for epistemological violence in psychology. (I'm not picking on psychology. Any kind of social

---

[2] This exercise may work best with a more focused subject – forensic psychology, testing psychology, etc. – that is specific to the interests of students.

science will have the potential for epistemological violence; psychology just happens to be what most of you are doing.) Reminder: epistemological violence, as conceptualized by Thomas Teo, happens when researchers choose to interpret data in ways that have negative consequences for a group of people (e.g., depicting them as inferior or dangerous), when equally plausible alternative explanations are available. Some questions that you might consider: *In psychology, what groups have been, or are likely to be, cast as inferior or dangerous? How have different groups been depicted in a negative light? What consequences for those groups have followed from how they have been represented in psychology? How could we avoid or limit epistemological violence in psychology?*

Your responses do not need to try and provide answers to all of these questions; these are only meant to help you think through the core question (instead, your responses should be your own thoughts on the core question). The core question that you should address in your responses is, *Where are the greatest dangers for epistemological violence in psychology and how can these be mitigated?* Your responses can be a stand-alone post of your thoughts on these questions or direct responses to your classmates (or both).

Reflection: How can I Respect my Participants?

Each week, you will be asked to write a reflection on the moral context of your research. These entries will ask you to consider the values that guide your research, the histories of, and potentials for, exploitation, injustice, or harm inherent in your research, the needs and vulnerabilities of those who participate in your research, and related questions.

As you write Study 2, think about the roles that study participants would play; about what would be expected of them and about what they would, and would not, be allowed to do. Now, reflect on the following questions and compose an entry that addresses them: *How can I ensure that my study participants are treated with respect (and civility)? Is there anything in my study design that might lead participants to feel disrespected? How can I acknowledge (and ensure that others acknowledge) and respect participants' unique values, beliefs, capabilities, and contributions? How can I ensure that participants can (and do) give full and ongoing consent to all aspects of their participation in my research?*

Assignment: Study 2

Week 10

Lecture: Qualitative Methods Overview
Lecture: Qualitative Standards

Exercise: Qualitative Standards
Readings: Qualitative Research in Psychology
Reflection: Who Bears the Costs of my Research?

Each week, you will be asked to write a reflection on the moral context of your research. These entries will ask you to consider the values that guide your research, the histories of, and potentials for, exploitation, injustice, or harm inherent in your research, the needs and vulnerabilities of those who participate in your research, and related questions.

As you work on designing Study 3, think about why you might do a study like this and about who it would benefit; about what resources (financial, political, interpersonal, etc.) it would take to complete the study and about who would provide those resources. Now, reflect on the following questions and compose an entry that addresses them: *What are the human, social, and institutional costs of my research and who is bearing them? Whose needs and values does my research serve? Whose needs or vulnerabilities might I miss or ignore in this research?*

Week 11

Lecture: Qualitative Research Practices
Exercise: Designing a Qualitative Data Collection Procedure
Reading: Example Qualitative Study
Reading: Choose Your Method
Reflection: Values in Data Analysis

Each week, you will be asked to write a reflection on the moral context of your research. These entries will ask you to consider the values that guide your research, the histories of, and potentials for, exploitation, injustice, or harm inherent in your research, the needs and vulnerabilities of those who participate in your research, and related questions.

As you design Study 3, think about the kinds of data you would collect and about how you would analyze those data; about what questions you would ask and about how you would determine the answers. Now, reflect on the following questions and compose an entry that addresses them: *Whose perspectives and values are represented in my interpretations of data? Whose perspectives and values have been marginalized, ignored, or silenced in my interpretations of data (whose voices have not been heard)?*

Week 12

Reading: Qualitative Reporting Standards

Levitt, H. M., Bamberg, M., Creswell, J. W., Frost, D. M., Josselson, R., and Suárez-Orozco, C. (2018). Journal Article Reporting Standards for Qualitative Primary, Qualitative Meta-Analytic, and Mixed Methods Research in Psychology: The APA Publications and Communications Board Task Force Report. *American Psychologist*, 73 (1), 26.

Exercise: Understanding Qualitative Research

One of the most debated questions in qualitative research is whether it is ethical or justifiable to combine or compare qualitative and quantitative methods. This is a debate because, historically, quantitative and qualitative researchers have viewed the purposes of research very differently (something you can see if you compare the standards and best practices for quantitative and qualitative methods). As the Giddings reading notes, some researchers have ignored this history and employed qualitative methods without an adequate understanding of their history or of their underlying assumptions. Thus, one of the essential responsibilities involved in doing qualitative research is to learn enough about these methods to employ them in a consistent and theoretically sophisticated way. This exercise and the reading linked above (Qualitative Reporting Standards) should give you a sense of how well you understand qualitative research and what you may still have to learn.

In this journal entry, answer each of the following questions: *What is the purpose of qualitative research? How do you justify it as valuable? How do you justify it as a contribution to science? How is it different from quantitative methods?*

Lecture: The Ethics of Intimacy
Exercise: The Ethics of Intimacy

In the lecture linked above, we discussed the following questions, adapted from Tuhiwai-Smith (2014):

How did you come to be here at the entry point of this community?

1) *Were you invited or did you select the community? What are the implications of being invited or doing the inviting?*
2) *What intellectual, emotional, ethical, political and spiritual preparation have you had?*
3) *Where have you come from? What are your geo-political origins and touchstones?*

What does this meeting mean for you?

1) *Is it the means to an end?*
2) *What baggage do you bring on to this space?*
3) *What hope and possibility do you bring on to this space?*

Who is your community?

1) *Who are your research ancestors?*
2) *Did they come here before? If so, what mark did they make?*
3) *How well do they represent your research to this new community (can they speak and sing?)?*

How do you "see" the people you are moving towards?

1) *Can you see them in their history and place?*
2) *Can you see their ancestors?*
3) *Can you see their baggage?*
4) *Can you see their hope and possibility?*

In this journal entry, do your best to answer these questions in the context of Study 3. You don't need to answer each question separately, but can give global answers that address the questions collectively.

Readings: Critical Questions for Qualitative Methods

Giddings, L. S. (2006). Mixed-Methods Research: Positivism Dressed in Drag? *Journal of Research in Nursing, 11* (3), 195–203. doi:10.1177/1744987106064635.

Smith, L. T. (2014). Social Justice, Transformation and Indigenous Methodologies. In R. E. Rinehart, K. N. Barbour, C. C. Pope, R. 0. Rinehart, K. 0. Barbour, and C. 0. Pope (eds.), *Ethnographic Worldviews: Transformations and Social Justice* (pp. 15–20). New York: Springer Science + Business Media. doi:10.1007/978-94-007-6916-8_2.

Reflection: Power in Research

Each week, you will be asked to write a reflection on the moral context of your research. These entries will ask you to consider the values that guide your research, the histories of, and potentials for, exploitation, injustice, or harm inherent in your research, the needs and vulnerabilities of those who participate in your research, and related questions.

As you write Study 3, think about all of the people who would be involved in this research; about their relationships to each other and to you. Now, reflect on the following questions and compose an entry that addresses them: *How could I acknowledge power differentials in my research collaborations or communities? Are these differences in power just? Do they reinforce existing social inequalities (long-standing inequalities based on race, gender, nationality, sexuality, etc.)? Could (and should) they be made more equal? How can I use my power or influence fairly?*

Assignment: Study 3

Week 13

Lecture: Research Ethics
Reading: Social Research Ethics
Exercise: My Responsibilities as a Researcher

In this exercise, I want you to reflect on your responsibilities to the different individuals or groups potentially impacted by your research. You can think about these responsibilities generally, but you should also reflect on the particular contexts of the three studies you designed for this class. Specifically, write a journal entry that outlines your responsibilities to: *your collaborators (lab members, assistants, etc.), your participants, the institutions where you conduct research (university, community partner, facility, etc.), the professions in whose journals the research will be published, and the broader community or society where that research will be applied.*

Lecture: The Institutional Context of Research
Readings: IRB Overview
Exercise: Consent Form

In this exercise, I want you to create a consent (or assent) form that could be used in one of the three studies you designed for this class. To create the consent form, look through the templates linked to this exercise and choose the one that best fits the circumstances of your study. Then use that template as the basis for your consent form, altering it to include information specific to your study. You can either upload the completed consent form as a separate document or paste it into the journal window below.

Reflection: What are my Responsibilities to my Collaborators?

Each week, you will be asked to write a reflection on the moral context of your research. These entries will ask you to consider the values that guide your research, the histories of, and potentials for, exploitation, injustice, or harm inherent in your research, the needs and vulnerabilities of those who participate in your research, and related questions.

As you consider the institutional context of research (ethics and grant review, participant pools, etc.), think about all of the people with whom you would need to collaborate to complete your research (lab members, research assistants, administrative staff, IRB specialists, etc.). Now, reflect on the following questions and compose an entry that addresses them: *What are my responsibilities to my collaborators? How do I treat them and how should I? Do I show them respect and collegiality? Do I act in good faith? What care do they need? What care can (and should) I give? Can they come to me for help? Am I worthy of their trust? Do I make their work easier (and what do I do that makes it harder)? Do I make their work better (and what do I do that makes it worse)?*

Week 14

Lecture: Choosing a Design
Exercise: Choosing a Design
Lecture: Planning and Preparing Research
Exercise: Planning a Thesis
Reflection: Planning Research Responsibly

Each week, you will be asked to write a reflection on the moral context of your research. These entries will ask you to consider the values that guide your research, the histories of, and potentials for, exploitation, injustice, or harm inherent in your research, the needs and vulnerabilities of those who participate in your research, and related questions.

As you consider the work involved in conducting a research project, think about all of the tasks (no matter how small) that you would need to complete before publishing a research report. Now, reflect on the following questions and compose an entry that addresses them: *What are my most important responsibilities in conducting research? Does the order and timing of my planning reflect those responsibilities? What commitments determine my planning priorities? Do these reflect my values (and those of my communities)?*

Assignment: Final Proposal

Appendix C
Questions to Aid Moral Reflection in Research Design

Mentored research activities are probably where most methods instruction takes place. Designing a specific curriculum for such activities, however, is a difficult task; mentoring is an uncertain and continually adaptive process resembling more an apprenticeship than a program of study. Thus, what follows is not a curriculum, but an intentionally open and adaptable tool for anyone, including new researchers, trying to think through the moral dilemmas and duties involved in research. Each heading below represents a question, dilemma, or design task about which someone seeking research mentorship might seek guidance. Below each heading is a set of questions (adapted from Part III of this book) that could be helpful in thinking through the dilemma or question posed in the heading.

I'd like to study ... (some topic, phenomenon, event, etc.)

Think of the research literature that you want to contribute to as a community that you will join. Who studies what you want to study? What do you know about them and about their work? What political causes have they, or their work, supported (or been used to support)? What values are reflected in their work? Now, or in the past, have they or the traditions they are part of, contributed to injustice, exploitation, discrimination, or harm? What kind of methods do they use? Will you feel good about using those kinds of methods? How do they treat others? What kinds of ideas do they use to support their work? Are you comfortable with those ideas? What are the written and unwritten rules in the communities and traditions where they work? Are you willing to be subject to those rules? Do those rules discriminate, obstruct, misrepresent, or harm? Are there things about those rules that you would change? How could you change them? Can you imagine any ways that research of the sort you want to do might be deployed politically (at any level)? Could those political uses involve purposes you find objectionable? Could the way you are framing your questions discriminate against, dehumanize, misrepresent, or hurt others? Why are your questions important? To whom, or for what purposes, are they important and what interests do they serve? Why should you (and the members of your research community) focus time and attention on those research questions (as opposed to other questions you or others might ask)? Are there other questions that you haven't considered or that might matter more to those from communities or traditions different form your own?

I'm working on a theory

When you picture the workings of your theory, whom do you imagine? Do you see yourself and those you care about, or someone else? How does your theory frame others? What kinds of persons (or other beings) does it imagine, allow, or valorize? What kinds does it exclude, demean, or pathologize? Why is your theory important? What values or ends will it serve? What are you trying to explain and who will use the knowledge you are seeking? How will they use it? Could your way of framing your theory be used to discriminate against, dehumanize, misrepresent, or hurt others? Who else has theories about the phenomena you want to study? How do those theories frame others? What are the goals and values reflected in or served by those theories? Whose goals, values, or interests are not represented in those theories? How has the knowledge produced from those theories been deployed? If you imagine yourself in a conversation with those other theorists, what would you say to them? What would you challenge? What would you accept?

I'm trying to figure out my design

[Many of the questions in other sections of this guide are useful for thinking through the moral affordances of design (questions about participants, space, equipment, etc.). In this section, I focus only on the most global questions, and refer the reader to the other sections for questions related to specific elements of design:]

Think of your study as a small community. What kind of community do you want it to be? What do you hope to achieve there? What do you hope will matter most to that community? What norms, rules, or standards do you think should guide that community? How will different design decisions promote (or interfere with) the kind of community you have imagined? Consider research that you have either read or participated in. How did those studies frame researchers, staff, and participants? What kinds of relationships did they produce? What norms, standards, or values did they reflect or promote? What design choices (choices about data types or forms of documentation, methods of control or manipulation, etc.) shaped these different research communities? How did these ways of framing research differ across different traditions of design? How have different design traditions been deployed historically? What political or cultural interests have they served? Who else will be part of your research community? What are your responsibilities to them? How have their voices, values, and interests been reflected in your design decisions? Who else will be impacted by what you do in your research? How have their values and interests been reflected in your design decisions?

I want to submit a grant application (or I need resources to run my study)

Why do you want a grant (or other resources)? Could you do your study without a grant or without access to extensive financial or insti-tutional resources? What conditions will you have to accept to get access to those resources? What compromises (in design, topic, pro-cedures, standards, etc.) will you have to make to meet those condi-tions? Will those compromises undermine your values, standards, or other commitments (moral and epistemic)? Will they undermine the commitments of those communities to which you belong and that you represent? Whose values or agendas might you be accepting when you accept certain resources? Where are those resources coming from and what values or agendas have been promoted by those who provide them? How will (or might) your research benefit, or be deployed by, those who provide those resources? Whose values, interests, needs, or vulnerabilities might be minimized or ignored because of the resource constraints you accept? Can you secure resources in a way that better supports or reflects your values and those of your communities? Who will bear the costs of your research; not just financial, but the costs of labor, risk, and the long-term impacts of your research? Are the voices and interests of those who are bearing the costs of your research reflected in the way you design, conduct, and deploy your research?

I need to recruit participants for my study (and/or submit an IRB proposal)

Think of participants in your research as invited guests. What duties do you have to those guests? Do your design decisions (including recruitment, scheduling, consent procedures, disclosure, and debriefing) reflect respect for those guests and consideration for their welfare? Is there any possibility that your research procedures might dehumanize, trivialize, alienate, objectify, or oppress participants in any way? Who are you inviting into your study? Do the participants you invite reflect the diversity of your communities, or of the world? Do the participants you invite belong to those groups most likely to benefit from your research? How can you ensure that your participants fully understand the nature and consequences of their participation in your research? How can you ensure that they can give full and ongoing consent to all aspects of their participation in your research? How will you assess and address the changing vulnerabilities and needs of your participants? What can you do to demonstrate respect for your participants' unique values, beliefs, capabilities, and contributions? How can you ensure that your participants have genuine opportunities to ask questions, raise objections, or seek redress? Are there ways that you could support participant self-advocacy? Are there ways that you could include participants in deliberations over risks, costs, and benefits? What would happen if you gave participants more influence over how your research is conducted? What could you do to help all participants feel safe (i.e., to feel that they will not be exploited, deceived, or hurt)? What will you do to ensure that all participants are safe?

I need a place to run (or host) my study

Think of your study as a small community. What kind of space do you want to create for that community? How do you hope others will feel when they participate in that community? How do you hope they will act? How will you treat strangers there? How will you treat guests? What kinds of places, and what kinds of dwelling practices, will contribute to the kind of space you want to make in your research?

How can these places and practices cultivate good will (among participants, administrative staff, assistants)? How can they build community? Are there ways that these could be exploitative, arrogant, dismissive, ungrateful, graceless, demanding, or entitled? Are there ways that these might either exploit or conserve physical, natural, and human resources? Will these places and practices ensure healthy environments? Will they permit long-term dwelling in (and use of) those environments? Will they support the well-being of those who participate in your research? Will they help your research community to sustain active, healthy research programs (to flourish and endure)? What kinds of spaces and dwelling practices do you see in the institutions and communities where you do your research? Are these responsible and consistent with what you and your communities value? Do they participate in a history of exploitation? How will those spaces and practices constrain your design choices? Are there ways to challenge or transform these?

I need equipment for my study (camera, webpage, self-report measure, computer, pipette)

Think about the furniture, tools, rooms, forms of documentation, instruments, measures, or devices that will be used in your research. What will your participants and fellow researchers have to learn for you to be able to use this equipment? How will their actions, experiences, attitudes, and bodies change when they use, or are subjected to the use of, this equipment? Will they understand and accept those changes before they occur? How have the kinds of equipment that you will use in your research already shaped persons, institutions, societies, and cultures? Is that history consistent with what you and your communities value? Do the kinds of equipment that you will use have a history of harm or exploitation? Does the nature of that equipment encourage deception, domination, hurt, or exploitation? How does that equipment frame persons, relationships, and groups? Is that framing consistent with how you understand persons, relationships, and groups? Is that framing consistent with your values and with those of your communities? Are there ways for you to use or create equipment that will better reflect your values and those of your communities?

There's so much to do

All research requires careful planning and organization. Think of that planning and organization as a statement about what you value (i.e., what is worth your time and attention). Of all the things you need to do to plan, prepare, and organize your study, which matter the most? What are your most important responsibilities? How can you ensure that the order and timing of your planning reflects those responsibilities? What would you need to change if you wanted to focus most, and soonest, on the things that you consider the most important? How are you deciding what matters most? Does that process reflect your values and those of your communities? How will you dispose of persons and their time in your planning? What will you do to understand their needs, capacities, and values? How can you make plans in a way that respects the needs, capacities, and values of others? How can you plan in a way that will sustain the energy and commitment of the members of your research community? How will the rules and requirements of the institutions where you conduct research constrain your planning and organization? Are these constraints consistent with your values? In what ways could you resist or influence these constraints?

I'm having trouble with … (assistants, lab members, the IRB manager)

Think of your study as a small community. What can you do to help that community function with good will and in good faith? Who do you rely on to complete your research? What are your responsibilities to those members of your research community? How have you treated them and how should you? What could you do to show them respect, collegiality, and good faith? What have you done (or might you do) to show them disrespect or bad faith? What care do they need? What care can (and should) you give? Can they come to you for help? Are you worthy of their trust? Do you make their work easier (and what do you do that makes it harder)? Do you make their work better (and what do you do that makes it worse)? Among those you rely on, who is most likely to be overlooked, ignored, or under-appreciated? What could you do to acknowledge power differentials in your research collaborations or communities? Are these differences in power just? Do they reinforce existing social inequalities (long-standing inequalities based on race, gender, nationality, sexuality, etc.)? Could (and should) they be made more equal? Do you use your power or influence unjustly? How will you fairly arbitrate disagreements? How will you respectfully and effectively respond to complaints, concerns, requests, or objections? Do your collaborators (and subordinates) feel like you have treated them fairly? Do they feel like you have used your influence responsibly?

I'm trying to figure out how to analyze my data

When you analyze data, you are making choices about what counts as knowledge, as well as choices about who gets to do the counting. How will you decide what kinds of data and what forms of analysis are valuable? What values determine those decisions? How are those values obscured in research writing and what could you do to make them explicit? Does everyone in your research community, or in your field, share those values or make those judgments in the same way? What forms of evidence or warrant have you not considered? What might be revealed or concealed if you considered different forms of evidence or warrant? How do the forms of analysis and types of data you use, as well as the conclusions you draw, frame persons and communities? How have these traditions of analysis and data collection been used in the past? Do they have a history of, or potential for, misuse or abuse? In those traditions, and in your interpretations, are individuals or groups derogated when other interpretations are possible? How could you challenge these histories and norms? In your study, who was involved in the collection and interpretation of data and how have they been treated (have they been respected, adequately compensated, and represented?)? Whose perspectives and values are represented in your interpretations? Whose perspectives and values have been marginalized, ignored, or silenced in your interpretations?

How do I write the report?

Think of your research report as a statement about who you are (as a research community), what you believe, what matters to you, and what you hope for. What can you do to make that report reflect your research community and the values of its members? How does your writing represent yourself and others? What does that writing hide, distort, suppress, or misrepresent? Does that writing obscure human dignity or agency, the moral qualities and complexities of research, or the perspectives of those in marginalized positions? How could that writing better reflect these qualities? How do disciplinary writing and reporting conventions constrain your writing? Do those conventions reflect what you and your communities value? How could you act to resist or transform those conventions? Who contributed to your research and to the report of that research? How will you make sure that the costs and rewards of authorship are equitably distributed? How will you ensure that those who conducted the research, wrote the reports, or contributed to the research in other ways, will receive credit and compensation for their work? Were the policies governing work and compensation made explicit to research workers and did they consent to these? Were these policies unfair, discriminatory, or exploitative in any way? What could you do to ensure fair policies in the production of your research reports? Did those who contributed to the research report have genuine opportunities to voice their concerns or to seek redress? How will you ensure that the perspectives and values of those who contributed to the research are fairly represented in the reporting? Whose perspectives did you emphasize in the writing of the report? Whose perspectives did you de-emphasize or ignore and why?

I'm trying to get my study published

Research publication is a collective labor organized within specific communities. Publishing is choosing both that work and that community. Who do you want to be in that community? Who do you want to read your work? Who do you think should have access to your work? Should anyone be denied access? How does your choice of publishing venue determine who will be denied access to your work? Do the publishing practices of the outlets where you submit your work reflect your values (and those of your communities)? Do those outlets support objectionable ideologies or engage in discriminatory or exploitative practices (including locking research behind egregious paywalls)? How could you influence those publishing practices? What responsibilities do you accept when you become part of a publishing community? How does your work in publishing, including editorial activities, shape what, and whose, perspectives are heard? How do you treat others in your editorial work? How could you support the review and editorial labor that sustains your research communities? How can you help ensure that this labor is fairly and sustainably compensated? Is your work reported or deployed in ways consistent with your values and those of your communities? Is your work reported or deployed in ways that harm or misrepresent others? How could you shape how your work is reported or deployed?

References

Adams, G., Dobles, I., Gómez, L. H., Kurtiş, T., & Molina, L. E. (2015). Decolonizing Psychological Science: Introduction to the Special Thematic Section. *Journal of Social and Political Psychology, 3(1)*, 213–238.

American Psychological Association. (2006). Policy Statement on Evidence-Based Practice in Psychology. *American Psychologist, 61*, 271–285.

American Psychological Association, Presidential Task Force on the Future of Psychology as a STEM Discipline. (2010). *Psychology as a core science, technology, engineering, and mathematics (STEM) discipline.* Retrieved from www.apa.org.

Banks, M. L., Czoty, P. W., & Negus, S. S. (2017). Utility of Nonhuman Primates in Substance Use Disorders Research. *ILAR Journal, 58 (2)*, 202–215.

Bazerman, C. (1988). *Shaping Written Knowledge: The Genre and Activity of the Experimental Article in Science* (vol. 356). University of Wisconsin Press.

Barenbaum, N. B., & Winter, D. G. (2003). Personality. In D. K. Freedheim and I. B. Weiner (eds.), *Handbook of Psychology* (pp. 177–204). John Wiley and Sons.

Benjamin, L. T. (2003). *Harry Hollingworth and the Shame of Applied Psychology.* Thick Description and Fine Texture: Studies in the History of Psychology (pp. 38–56).

Bernstein, R. J. (1983). *Beyond Objectivism and Relativism: Science, Hermeneutics, and Praxis.* University of Pennsylvania Press.

Bhatia, S. (2019). Searching for Justice in an Unequal World: Reframing Indigenous Psychology as a Cultural and Political Project. *Journal of Theoretical and Philosophical Psychology, 39 (2)*, 107.

Bibace, R., Clegg, J. W., & Valsiner, J. (2009). What's in a Name? Understanding the Implications of Participant Terminology. *Integrative Psychological and Behavioral Science, 43 (1)*, 67–77.

Billig, M. (2011). Writing Social Psychology: Fictional Things and Unpopulated Texts. *British Journal of Social Psychology, 50 (1)*, 4–20.

Blum, D. (1996). *The Monkey Wars.* Oxford University Press.

Bromberg, W., & Simon, F. (1968). The "Protest" Psychosis: A Special Type of Reactive Psychosis. *Archives of General Psychiatry, 19* (2), 155–160.

Brinkmann, S. (2004). The Topography of Moral Ecology. *Theory & Psychology, 14* (1), 57–80.

Brydon-Miller, M. (2001). Education, Research, and Action Theory and Methods of Participatory. In D. L. Tolman and M. B. Miller (eds.), *From Subjects to Subjectivities: A Handbook of Interpretive and Participatory Methods* (pp. 76–89). New York University Press.

Burman, E. (2006). Emotions and Reflexivity in Feminised Education Action Research. *Educational Action Research, 14* (3), 315–332.

(2012). Disciplines for and against Psychology. *Universitas Psychologica, 11* (2), 645–662.

Chataway, C. J. (2001). Negotiating the Observer–Observed Relationship. In D. L. Tolman and M. B. Miller (eds.), *From Subjects to Subjectivities: A Handbook of Interpretive and Participatory Methods* (pp. 239–255). New York University Press.

Clegg, J. W. (2010). Uncertainty as a Fundamental Scientific Value. *Integrative Psychological and Behavioral Science, 44* (3), 245–251.

(2016). Reconsidering Philosophy of Science Pedagogy in Psychology: An Evaluation of Methods Texts. *Journal of Theoretical and Philosophical Psychology, 36* (4), 199–213.

(2019). The Moral Affordances of Publishing Practices. In B. D. Slife and S. Yanchar (eds.), *Hermeneutic Moral Realism in Psychology: Theory and Practice* (pp. 86–96). Routledge.

Clegg, J. W., & Slife, B. D. (2005). Epistemology and the Hither Side: A Levinasian Account of Relational Knowing. *European Journal of Psychotherapy & Counselling, 7* (1–2), 65–76.

Clegg, J. W., Wiggins, B. J., & Ostenson, J. A. (2020). Overpublication as a Symptom of Audit Culture: A Comment on Phaf (2020). *Theory & Psychology, 30* (2), 292–298.

Collins, H. (2010). *Tacit and Explicit Knowledge.* University of Chicago Press.

Danziger, K. (1990). *Constructing the Subject: Historical Origins of Psychological Research.* Cambridge University Press.

Daston, L., & Galison, P. (2007). *Objectivity.* Zone Books.

Deneau, G., Yanagita, T., & Seevers, M. H. (1969). Self-Administration of Psychoactive Substances by the Monkey. *Psychopharmacologia, 16* (1), 30–48.

Dewsbury, D. A. (2003). Conflicting Approaches: Operant Psychology Arrives at a Primate Laboratory. *The Behavior Analyst, 26* (2), 253–265.

Dowling, M. (2006). Approaches to Reflexivity in Qualitative Research. *Nurse Researcher, 13* (3).

Duffy, M., & Chenail, R. J. (2009). Values in Qualitative and Quantitative Research. *Counseling and Values, 53 (1)*, 22–38.

Feyerabend, P. (1987). *Farewell to Reason.* Verso.

(1993). *Against Method.* Verso.

Fine, M. (2016). Just Methods in Revolting Times. *Qualitative Research in Psychology, 13 (4)*, 347–365.

Finlay, L. (2002). Negotiating the Swamp: The Opportunity and Challenge of Reflexivity in Research Practice. *Qualitative Research, 2 (2)*, 209–230.

Fuller, S. (2000). *The Governance of Science.* Open Press.

Gadamer, H. G. (1975b). *Truth and Method.* Seabury Press.

Gilbert, G. N., & Mulkay, M. (1984). *Opening Pandora's Box: A Sociological Analysis of Scientists' Discourse.* Cambridge University Press.

Gilligan, C. (1982). *In a Different Voice.* Harvard University Press.

Gluck, J. P. (2016, September 2). Second thoughts of an animal researcher. *The New York Times.* Retrieved from www.nytimes.com.

Goldman, A. (1999). *Knowledge in a Social World.* Oxford University Press.

Gone, J. P. (2011). Is Psychological Science A-Cultural? *Cultural Diversity and Ethnic Minority Psychology, 17 (3)*, 234.

Guillemin, M., & Gillam, L. (2004). Ethics, Reflexivity, and "Ethically Important Moments" in Research. *Qualitative Inquiry, 10 (2)*, 261–280.

Haan, N., Bellah, R. N., Rabinow, P., & Sullivan, W. M. (1983). *Social Science as Moral Inquiry.* Columbia University Press.

Hacker, P. M. S. (2015). Philosophy and Scientism: What Cognitive Neuroscience Can, and What it Cannot, Explain. In R. N. Williams and D. N. Robinson (eds.), *Scientism: The New Orthodoxy* (pp. 97–116). Bloomsbury Publishing.

Halling, S., Kunz, G., & Rowe, J. O. (1994). The Contributions of Dialogal Psychology to Phenomenological Research. *Journal of Humanistic Psychology Special Issue: Dialogue, 34 (1)*, 109–131.

Haney, C., Banks, W. C., & Zimbardo, P. G. (1973). A Study of Prisoners and Guards in a Simulated Prison. *Naval Research Reviews, 9*, 1–17.

Haraway, D. (1987). A Manifesto for Cyborgs: Science, Technology, and Socialist Feminism in the 1980s. *Australian Feminist Studies, 2 (4)*, 1–42.

Harding, S. (1992). After the Neutrality Ideal: Science, Politics, and "Strong Objectivity." *Social Research*, 567–587.

Head, J. C., Quigua, F., & Clegg, J. W. (2019). The Radical Potentials of Human Experience: Maslow, Leary, and the Prehistory of Qualitative Inquiry. *Qualitative Psychology, 6 (1)*, 116.

Heidegger, M. (1962). *Being and Time (J. Macquarrie & E. Robinson, trans.)*. Basil Blackwell.

(1993). *Basic Writings: Revised and Expanded*, ed. D. F. Krell. Harper Collins.

Henrich, J., Heine, S. J., & Norenzayan, A. (2010). Most People Are Not WEIRD. *Nature, 466 (7302)*, 29–29.

Herrnstein, R. J., & Murray, C. (1995). *The Bell Curve: Intelligence and Class Structure in American Life*. Simon and Schuster.

Hook, D., Kiguwa, P., & Mkhize, N. (2004). *Critical Psychology*. UCT Press.

Howard, D. (2009). Better Red than Dead – Putting an End to the Social Irrelevance of Postwar Philosophy of Science. *Science & Education, 18 (2)*, 199–220.

Jahoda, M., Lazarsfeld, P. F., & Zeisel, H. (2002). *Marienthal: The Sociography of an Unemployed Community*. Transaction Publishers.

Jasanoff, S. (2005). In the Democracies of DNA: Ontological Uncertainty and Political Order in Three States. *New Genetics and Society, 24 (2)*, 139–156.

(2011). *Designs on Nature: Science and Democracy in Europe and the United States*. Princeton University Press.

Jensen, A. (1969). How Much Can We Boost IQ and Scholastic Achievement? *Harvard Educational Review, 39 (1)*, 1–123.

Keller, E. F. (1983). *A Feeling for the Organism: The Life and Work of Barbara McClintock*. W. H. Freeman & Co.

Kitcher, P. (2003). *Science, Truth, and Democracy*. Oxford University Press.

Knorr-Cetina, K. (1981) *The Manufacture of Knowledge. An Essay on the Constructivist and Contextual Nature of Science*. Pergamon Press.

Koch, S. (1973). The Image of Man in Encounter Groups. *The American Scholar*, 636–652.

(1981). The Nature and Limits of Psychological Knowledge: Lessons of a Century Qua "Science." *American Psychologist, 36 (3)*, 257–269.

Kraft, A. (2015, December 14). NIH to stop baby monkey experiments. *CBS News*. Retrieved from www.cbsnews.com.

Kuhn, T. S. (1970). *The Structure of Scientific Revolutions (2nd enl. ed.)*. University of Chicago Press.

Latour, B. (2004). Why Has Critique Run Out of Steam? From Matters of Fact to Matters of Concern. *Critical Inquiry, 30 (2)*, 225–248.

Latour, B., & Woolgar, S. (1986). *Laboratory Life: The Construction of Scientific Facts*. Princeton University Press.

Levinas, E. (1969). *Totality and Infinity* (A. Lingis, trans.). Duquesne University Press (original work published 1961).

(1997). *Otherwise Than Being: Or Beyond Essence* (A. Lingis, trans.). Duquesne University Press (original work published 1981).

Levitt, H. M., Bamberg, M., Creswell, J. W., Frost, D. M., Josselson, R., & Suárez-Orozco, C. (2018). Journal Article Reporting Standards for Qualitative Primary, Qualitative Meta-Analytic, and Mixed Methods Research in Psychology: The APA Publications and Communications Board Task Force Report. *American Psychologist, 73* (1), 26.

Livingston, E. (1999). Cultures of Proving. *Social Studies of Science, 29,* 867–888.

Lomax, E. (1977). The Laura Spelman Rockefeller Memorial: Some of its Contributions to Early Research in Child Development. *Journal of the History of the Behavioral Sciences, 13* (3), 283–293.

Longino, H. E. (1995). Gender, Politics, and the Theoretical Virtues. *Synthese, 104* (3), 383–397.

(2002). *The Fate of Knowledge.* Princeton University Press.

Lovasz, N., & Clegg, J. W. (2019). The Social Production of Evidence in Psychology: A Case Study of the APA Task Force on Evidence-Based Practice. In K. O'Doherty, L. Osbeck, E. Schraube, and J. Yen (eds.), *Psychological Studies of Science and Technology* (pp. 213–235). Palgrave Macmillan.

Lynch, M. (1999). Silence in Context: Ethnomethodology and Social Theory. *Human Studies, 22,* 211–233.

Magwaza, A. (2001). Submissions to the South African Truth and Reconciliation Commission: The Reflections of a Commissioner on the Culpability of Psychology. In N. Duncan, A. van Niekerk, C. de la Rey, and M. Seedat (eds.), *"Race," Racism, Knowledge Production and Psychology in South Africa* (pp. 37–59). Nova Science Publishers.

Marecek, J., Kimmel, E. B., Crawford, M., & Hare-Mustin, R. T. (2003). Psychology of Women and Gender. In D. K. Freedheim and I. B. Weiner (eds.), *Handbook of Psychology* (pp. 249–268). John Wiley and Sons.

Maslow, A. H. (1966). *The Psychology of Science: A Reconnaissance.* Harper and Row.

Melchert, T. P. (2016). Leaving Behind our Preparadigmatic Past: Professional Psychology as A Unified Clinical Science. *American Psychologist, 71* (6), 486–496.

Morawski, J. (2001a). Gifts Bestowed, Gifts Withheld: Assessing Psychological Theory with a Kochian Attitude. *American Psychologist, 56* (5), 433.

(2001b). Feminist Research Methods: Bringing Culture to Science. In Tolman, D. L. and Miller, M. B. (eds.), *From Subjects to Subjectivities: A Handbook of Interpretive and Participatory Methods* (pp. 57–75). New York University Press.

(2011). Our Debates: Finding, Fixing, and Enacting Reality. *Theory & Psychology, 21* (2), 260–274.

(2015). Epistemological Dizziness in the Psychology Laboratory: Lively Subjects, Anxious Experimenters, and Experimental Relations, 1950–1970. *Isis, 106* (3), 567–597.

(2019). The Replication Crisis: How Might Philosophy and Theory of Psychology Be of Use? *Journal of Theoretical and Philosophical Psychology, 39* (4), 218.

Niaz, M. (2010). Science Curriculum and Teacher Education: The Role of Presuppositions, Contradictions, Controversies and Speculations vs Kuhn's "Normal Science." *Teaching and Teacher Education, 26* (4), 891–899.

Nicholas, L. J. (2014). A History of South African (SA) Psychology. *Universitas Psychologica, 13 (SPE5),* 1983–1991.

Noddings, N. (2013). *Caring: A Relational Approach to Ethics and Moral Education.* University of California Press.

Nosek, B. A., Aarts, A. A., Anderson, J. E., Kappes, H. B., & Open Science Collaboration. (2015). Estimating the Reproducibility of Psychological Science. *Science, 349* (6251).

Nosek, B. A., Spies, J. R., & Motyl, M. (2012). Scientific Utopia: II. Restructuring Incentives and Practices to Promote Truth over Publishability. *Perspectives on Psychological Science, 7* (6), 615–631.

O'Reilly, M., Parker, N., & Hutchby, I. (2011). Ongoing Processes of Managing Consent: The Empirical Ethics of Using Video-Recording in Clinical Practice and Research. *Clinical Ethics, 6* (4), 179–185.

Osbeck, L. (2018). *Values in Psychological Science: Re-imagining Epistemic Priorities at a New Frontier.* Cambridge University Press.

Ostenson, J. A., Clegg, J. W., & Wiggins, B. J. (2017). Industrialized Higher Education and its Sustainable Alternatives. *The Review of Higher Education, 40* (4), 509–532.

Padovani, F., Richardson, A., & Tsou, J. Y. (eds.) (2015). *Objectivity in Science: New Perspectives from Science and Technology Studies. Boston Studies in the Philosophy and History of Science, 310.* Springer.

Peirce, C. (1935). Principles of Philosophy. In C. Hartshorne & P. Weiss (eds.), *Collected Papers of Charles Sanders Peirce.* Harvard University Press.

Pelham, B. W., & Blanton, H. (2007). *Conducting Research in Psychology: Measuring the Weight of Smoke.* Thomson Wadsworth.

Peterson, D. (2015). All That Is Solid: Bench-building at the Frontiers of Two Experimental Sciences. *American Sociological Review, 80* (6), 1201–1225.

(2016). The Baby Factory: Difficult Research Objects, Disciplinary Standards, and the Production of Statistical Significance. *Socius, 2,* DOI: 10.1177/2378023115625071.

Phillips, N. (2014, July 31). University of Wisconsin to reprise controversial monkey studies. *Wisconsin Watch*. Retrieved from www .wisconsinwatch.org.

Plato. (1981). *Five Dialogues*. (G.M.A. Grube, trans.). Hackett Publishing Company.

Polanyi, M. (1958). *Personal Knowledge: Towards a Post-critical Philosophy*. University of Chicago Press.

Proctor, R. N. (1991). *Value-free Science? Purity and Power in Modern Knowledge*. Harvard University Press.

Pryiomka, K., & Clegg, J. W. (2020). A Historical Overview of Psychological Inquiry as a Contested Method. In W. Pickren (ed.), *Oxford Research Encyclopedia of Psychology*. Oxford University Press.

Rabinow, P. (1983). Humanism as Nihilism: The Bracketing of Truth and Seriousness in American Cultural Anthropology. In N. Haan, R. N. Bellah, P. Rabinow, & W. M. Sullivan (eds.), *Social Science as Moral Inquiry* (pp. 52–75). Columbia University Press.

Richardson, F. C., Fowers, B. J., & Guignon, C. B. (1999). *Re-envisioning Psychology: Moral Dimensions of Theory and Practice*. Jossey-Bass.

Roediger, H., III (2004). What Should They Be Called? *Observer, 17* (4), 5, 46–48.

Rogers, A. (2017). *Star neuroscientist Tom Insel leaves the Google-spawned verily for... a Startup*. Wired. Retrieved from www. wired. com/.

Rose, A. C. (2011). The Invention of Uncertainty in American Psychology: Intellectual Conflict and Rhetorical Resolution, 1890–1930. *History of Psychology, 14* (4), 356.

Rosnow, R. L., & Rosenthal, R. (2008). *Beginning Behavioral Research: A Conceptual Primer*. Pearson/Prentice Hall.

Rushton, J. P. (1995). *Race, Evolution, and Behavior: A Life History Perspective*. Transaction Publishers.

Principe, L. M. (2015). Scientism and the Religion of Science. In D. N. Robinson and R. N. Williams (eds.), *Scientism: The New Orthodoxy* (pp. 41–61). Bloomsbury Academic.

Seedat, M. (1998). A Characterisation of South African Psychology (1948–1988): The Impact of Exclusionary Ideology. *South African Journal of Psychology, 28* (2), 74–84.

Shore, C. (2008). Audit Culture and Illiberal Governance. *Anthropological Theory, 8* (3), 278–298.

Sokal, M. M. (2010). Scientific Biography, Cognitive Deficits, and Laboratory Practice: James McKeen Cattell and Early American Experimental Psychology, 1880–1904. *Isis, 101* (3), 531–554.

Solomon, M. (2008). STS and Social Epistemology of Science. In E. J. Hackett, O. Amsterdamska, M. Lynch, and J. Wajcman (eds.), *The*

Handbook of Science and Technology Studies (pp. 241–258). MIT Press.

Sugarman, J. (2015). Neoliberalism and Psychological Ethics. *Journal of Theoretical and Philosophical Psychology, 35* (2), 103–116.

Sugarman, J., & Thrift, E. (2017). Neoliberalism and the Psychology of Time. *Journal of Humanistic Psychology,* DOI: 10.1177/0022167817716686.

Smith, J. K. (1993). *After the Demise of Empiricism: The Problem of Judging Social and Educational Inquiry.* Ablex Publishing Corporation.

Smith, J. K. A. (2015). Science as Cultural Performance: Leveling the Playing Field in the Theology and Science Conversation. In R. N. Williams and D. N. Robinson (eds.), *Scientism: The New Orthodoxy* (pp. 177–191). Bloomsbury Academic.

Smith, L. T. (2013). Social Justice, Transformation and Indigenous Methodologies. In R. E. Rinehart, K. N. Barbour, and C. C. Pope (eds.) *Ethnographic Worldviews: Transformations and Social Justice* (pp. 15–20). Springer Science & Business Media.

Stewart, A. J., & Shields, S. A. (2001). Gatekeepers as Change Agents: What Are Feminist Psychologists Doing in Places Like This. In Tolman, D. L. and Miller, M. B. (eds.), *From Subjects to Subjectivities: A Handbook of Interpretive and Participatory Methods* (pp. 304–319). New York University Press.

Taylor, C. A. (1996). *Defining Science.* University of Wisconsin Press.

Teo, T. (2010). What is Epistemological Violence in the Empirical Social Sciences? *Social and Personality Psychology Compass, 4* (5), 295–303.

(2015). Are Psychological "Ethics Codes" Morally Oblique? *Journal of Theoretical and Philosophical Psychology, 35* (2), 78.

Thompson, R. F., & Zola, S. M. (2003). Biological Psychology. In D. K. Freedheim and I. B. Weiner (eds.), *Handbook of Psychology* (pp. 47–66). John Wiley and Sons.

Trafimow, D., & Marks, M. (2016). Editorial. *Basic and Applied Social Psychology, 38,* 1–2.

Traweek, S. (1988). *Beamtimes and Lifetimes: The World of High Energy Physicists.* Harvard University Press.

Tuval-Mashiach, R. (2017). Raising the Curtain: The Importance of Transparency in Qualitative Research. *Qualitative Psychology, 4* (2), 126.

Tweney, R. D., & Budzynski, C. A. (2000). The Scientific Status of American Psychology in 1900. *American Psychologist, 55* (9), 1014.

van Fraasen, B. C. (2015). Naturalism in Epistemology. In D. N. Robinson and R. N. Williams (eds.), *Scientism: The New Orthodoxy* (pp. 63–95). Bloomsbury Academic.

Vasquez, M. J. (2012). Psychology and Social Justice: Why We Do What We Do. *American Psychologist, 67* (5), 337.

Walsh, R. T. (2015). Bending the Arc of North American Psychologists' Moral Universe toward Communicative Ethics and Social Justice. *Journal of Theoretical and Philosophical Psychology, 35* (2), 90.

Weisstein, N. (1993). Power Resistance and Science: A Call for a Revitalized Feminist Psychology. *Feminism & Psychology, 3* (2), 239–245.

Wiggins, B. J. (2011). Confronting the Dilemma of Mixed Methods. *Journal of Theoretical and Philosophical Psychology, 31* (1), 44.

Wiggins, B. J., & Christopherson, C. D. (2019). The Replication Crisis in Psychology: An Overview for Theoretical and Philosophical Psychology. *Journal of Theoretical and Philosophical Psychology, 39,* 202–217.

Williams, R. N. (2015). Introduction. In R. N. Williams and D. N. Robinson (eds.), *Scientism: The New Orthodoxy* (pp. 1–21). Bloomsbury Academic.

Winston, A. S. (1998). Science in the Service of the Far Right: Henry E. Garrett, the IAAEE, and the Liberty Lobby. *Journal of Social Issues, 54* (1), 179–210.

Young, J. L. (2013). A Brief History of Self-report in American Psychology. In J. W. Clegg (ed.), *Self-observation in the Social Sciences* (pp. 45–65). Transaction.

Index

CPSIA information can be obtained
at www.ICGtesting.com
Printed in the USA
BVHW042333110122
626010BV00009B/53

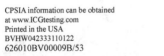

9 781009 011129